PIVOTAL
MOMENTS
IN HISTORY

THE FALL OF THE
ROMAN EMPIRE

BY RITA J. MARKEL

TWENTY-FIRST CENTURY BOOKS
MINNEAPOLIS

To Eileen, Al, and John

Consultant: Oliver Nicholson, M.A., D.Phil., Assistant Professor of Classical and Near Eastern Studies, University of Minnesota

Primary source material in this text is printed over an antique-paper texture.

The image on the jacket and cover is of Marcus Aurelius and the surrender of the Germanic tribes, which is a scene on the Arch of Constantine in Rome, ca. A.D. 315.

Twenty-First Century Books
A division of Lerner Publishing Group, Inc.
241 First Avenue North
Minneapolis, MN 55401 U.S.A.

Website address: www.lernerbooks.com

Library of Congress Cataloging-in-Publication Data

Markel, Rita J.
    The fall of the Roman Empire / by Rita J. Markel.
        p.   cm. — (Pivotal moments in history)
    Includes bibliographical references and index.
    ISBN 978-0-8225-5919-1 (lib. bdg. : alk. paper)
    1. Rome—History—Empire, 284-476—Juvenile literature 2. Rome—History— Germanic Invasions, 3rd–6th centuries—Juvenile literature. I. Title.
DG311.M367 2008
937'.06—dc22   2006100918

Manufactured in the United States of America
1 2 3 4 5 6 – DP – 13 12 11 10 09 08

CONTENTS

CHAPTER ONE

GLORY DAYS

"Civus Romanus Sum—
I am a Roman citizen."

—*Cicero, first century* B.C.

In A.D. 9, Quintilius Varus, a general of the Roman army, led his men into a deadly ambush. During the next three days, as many as 27,000 soldiers of the early Roman Empire were killed in battle. Their bodies were found mutilated, their heads nailed to trees. It was one of the worst military disasters of the ancient world. The Romans had been caught off guard in the dark Teutoburg Forest, part of modern-day Germany. The

Roman emperor Octavian had sent his soldiers there to push the German tribes—or, as the Romans called them, barbarians—farther from the empire's borders. But the German tribes had joined forces and attacked before the Romans could strike. Leading the attack was Arminius, a former Roman soldier and citizen, but a barbarian by birth. He had organized the warriors after going home and seeing the extreme poverty his own people endured on the borders of the Roman Empire. He blamed the Romans for the suffering he saw.

A scupture of the Roman emperor Octavian

Quintilius Varus committed suicide rather than be taken prisoner by the barbarians. But the enemy found his body, cut off the head, and sent it back to Rome, the empire's capital city. Stunned by this defeat, Octavian is said to have banged his head against a wall repeatedly, crying out, "Quintilius Varus . . . give me back my men!"

Surprisingly, Octavian decided not to force the barbarians back to the northern seas, seize their land, and extend the empire. Instead, he decided to defend the territory he had, leaving the barbarians on the Roman borders. Some historians believe that this decision doomed the empire.

Because of the ongoing threat to its borders, the Roman Empire had to continuously guard its frontier. As a result, the empire's human and financial resources dwindled. In the end, the barbarians destroyed the glory that was once Rome. This is one theory of how the Roman Empire fell. There are others, including those that say the empire didn't really fall. It just changed into different disconnected units. Historians disagree on exactly what happened to the empire. But most accept that A.D. 476 was a pivotal moment in world history as the Roman Empire after that year was very different from what it had been in earlier times.

A WILL TO CONQUER

In the ninth century B.C., long before it became an empire, Rome was just a small village on the Italian peninsula. By the 600s B.C., the Romans were ruled by the powerful Etruscan monarchy. But in the early 500s B.C., the Romans rebelled and formed a republic.

In theory, the republic gave average Romans a voice in their government. In reality, the republic was controlled by the Senate, which decided on the laws and policies of the state. The Senate was made up of a small number of wealthy, upper-class men who owned land. It was these men whose voices were heard. The poor were silent.

Rome developed from a city into a powerful self-governing state that expanded throughout the Italian

This undated engraving shows a session of the Roman Senate. Roman senators were wealthy men who owned land.

peninsula. As it grew in military power, Rome took over the lands bordering the Mediterranean Sea and beyond. The gap between rich and poor grew with the empire. Victorious military leaders became extremely wealthy from plunder (goods seized from defeated peoples) and the sale of captives as slaves. The profits made from the sale of supplies and weapons to Rome's busy army went to a few select families who were already the richest and most powerful in Roman society. The wealthy were given positions of power that brought personal gain in the newly conquered lands. This ensured their future wealth.

However, Rome's growth opened some doors for the poor, as well. With expansion, commerce grew and a middle class developed. In addition, the military offered new opportunities to people from the lower level of society. At first, the Roman army had been a part-time operation, made up of landowning citizens who served for short periods of time. These men voluntarily performed their service, seeing it as a duty and an honor. But as Rome conquered distant lands, periods of military service grew much longer. It became clear that Rome needed a full-time, professional army. The government recruited soldiers from Rome's poor and gave them excellent training. These men became Rome's legionaries, who became known for their dedication and discipline. The Romans also recruited from their conquered provinces. These men became auxiliaries, or helpers, to the regular army.

This first-century A.D. pavement mosaic shows Roman soldiers with shields. The Roman army changed from a volunteer army to a full-time professional army during the first century B.C. and into the first century A.D.

In addition to wealth, military generals gained great power. To increase it, they began fighting one another. These power struggles led to civil wars that threw the Roman Republic into years of turmoil. The republic could not simultaneously control an army big enough to conquer other lands and keep its generals from using their troops to compete with one another. Hoping to end the chaos caused by the power struggles, the Senate decided to give control to one man, Octavian, a statesman and highly successful general. In 27 B.C., Octavian became the republic's first real emperor and was given the title of Augustus, meaning "the revered" or "highly regarded one." But Octavian gave himself a more modest title, First Citizen.

FROM REPUBLIC TO EMPIRE

Octavian shrewdly kept the outward appearance of the republic. He allowed the Senate to continue to meet, but he quietly stripped away its power. The senators were still very important men, but they no longer ran the government and never would again. The government had changed from a republic to an empire, with a single supreme leader—one who needed the army in order to stay in power.

In addition to the power to rule, the Senate gave Octavian control of Rome's justice system. Along with later emperors, he became Rome's highest legal authority. The emperors were free to issue edicts (commands) to the people. But all Roman citizens were protected by a common system of law. This system guaranteed every citizen certain rights, such as the right to a trial when charged with a crime and the right to defend

WHO WAS OCTAVIAN?

In The Aeneid, written in 19 B.C., the poet Virgil portrays Octavian as a descendant of Roman mythic characters. But, in fact, Octavian was born to a noble Roman family in 63 B.C. and was later named Gaius Julius Caesar Octavianus (known simply as Octavian). He was emperor of the Roman Empire from 27 B.C. until his death in A.D. 14. From the outset, Octavian ruled with humility and caution. He was especially careful to show public respect for the Senate. He was, after all, the nephew, adopted son, and heir of Julius Caesar. Caesar had been assassinated in 44 B.C. for challenging the Senate's authority.

himself in court. (Women were not granted citizenship, although they did have a few rights.) The Roman legal system was flexible. It could be changed to accommodate the different customs and attitudes of people throughout the empire.

The fact that the republic was now a dictatorship probably didn't bother most Romans. This was because under Octavian, the Pax Romana, or Roman Peace (27 B.C.–A.D. 180), began. In modern times, this period of "peace" might not seem so peaceful at all. There were uprisings, assassinations, and internal power struggles, as well as battles with warring tribes along the empire's borders. But when Roman citizens compared the reign of Octavian to the chaos of the civil wars, most agreed that this was indeed an era of peace and prosperity. By the time the emperor Trajan ended his reign in A.D. 117, Rome had grown from a city-state of 10,000 people to an empire of as many as 100 million people. Its territory extended beyond the Italian peninsula to all the lands bordering the Mediterranean Sea, north through the European continent to the British Isles, and east to the Persian Gulf. Its total land mass was about 3,500,000 square miles (9,000,000 square kilometers)—about the size of the continental United States.

TAXATION

To pay for its growth, the early Roman republic taxed its citizens. These taxes, based on wealth and property, were very low. If the government had extra money, the taxpayers got a refund. As the empire grew, it stopped taxing native Roman citizens and instead taxed the people of the conquered provinces. Until Octavian's rule, taxes were collected in the provinces by tax farmers. These wealthy Romans could pay the taxes out of their own funds and then collect payments from the people after crops were harvested. But the tax farmers collected more money than they paid out and made huge profits. This was unfair to the people in the provinces. To fix this problem, Octavian regulated the tax system. He stopped the practice of tax farming and ordered a census, or a count, of the people. Once he knew how many taxpayers there were, he set a tax based on each individual's income for that year. This made the tax system fair and kept it honest.

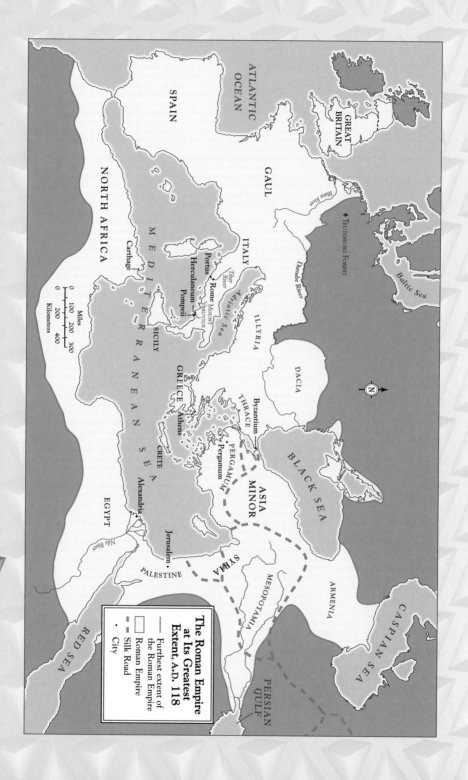

The Roman Empire
at Its Greatest
Extent, A.D. 118

— Furthest extent of
the Roman Empire
Roman Empire
Silk Road
• City

THE MILITARY

To exist, the empire needed a strong military. By the early first century B.C., the Romans had two large naval fleets. These forces, along with smaller groups of ships, were based along the empire's coasts. Their sailors moved battle troops, fought pirates, and guarded the ports and grain supplies. These were all important roles in protecting the realm's interests. But the heart of the empire was always the army.

By the time of the Pax Romana, the army's legionaries, or foot soldiers, were at their best. These soldiers were well-trained, quickly mobilized, and extremely dedicated to the empire. Under Octavian, the legionaries were divided into

This relief from Trajan's column in Rome, created in the early second century A.D., portrays legionaries geting ready to embark on ships.

twenty-eight legions, each of which had about 50,000 men. The legions were made up of smaller units, called centuries. Although their name means one hundred, centuries could consist of anywhere from 80 to 160 men.

Roman soldiers were skilled at hand-to-hand combat. In a group, they were an effective killing machine. One of their most successful battle strategies was called the tortoise. As they advanced on an enemy fortification, the legionaries locked their shields together over their heads to create a "shell." With the shell in place, they could approach, or even penetrate, a highly fortified target, such as a walled city. Enemy soldiers standing on the wall or on platforms overhead could not pierce the shell with their weapons.

A Jewish historian, Josephus, described the strict training of the Roman army in a letter from around A.D. 66. This was during the emperor Vespasian's campaign against Jews on the Mediterranean's eastern coast. Josephus wrote:

Reenactors demonstrate the Roman army's tortoise technique.

By their military exercises the Romans instill into their soldiers fortitude not only of body but also of soul; fear, too, plays its part in their training. For they have laws which punish with death not merely desertion but even a slight neglect of duty. . . . This perfect discipline . . . welds the men into a single body, so compact are their ranks, so alert their movements . . . so quick their ears for orders, their eyes for signals, their hands for tasks.

When they were victorious, the Romans were not modest. Josephus gave an eyewitness account of the army's victory march in A.D. 71, after the Romans had defeated the Jews. He described the bright silk robes and crowns of laurel leaves worn by the military leaders as they stood on a platform overlooking a huge crowd. Everyone in the city came to watch. The soldiers had been in formation since before dawn. They stood at attention, as prayers were offered to their gods. Then came a procession of carriages to transport the heroes toward the city's theaters. Everyone could see and hail them as victors. Josephus wrote:

It is impossible adequately to describe the multitudes of those spectacles and their magnificence . . . for the . . . exhibition . . . of almost everything that men have ever been blessed by fortune . . . is displayed [by] the majesty of the Roman Empire.

But even with such celebrations and bonuses from their officers, soldiers had a tough life. Ordinary legionaries were required to sign up for long periods—often decades. Then, if they were still needed, soldiers served even more time as reserves. Sometimes they were sent far from their homes and families. And until A.D. 97, soldiers could not legally marry.

Helping the Roman legions were the auxiliary soldiers, hired from the lands that the army conquered. Romans looked for auxiliaries who had special skills perfected by their own people. For example, they hired archers from Crete and Syria and fearless horsemen from Gaul (Europe). These auxiliaries became an important part of the army. When they finished their army service, they became Roman citizens.

The most elite soldiers in the army, however, were the Praetorian Guards. They were made up almost entirely of men from the Italian peninsula. They were the emperor's trusted personal guard and always went with him on his military campaigns.

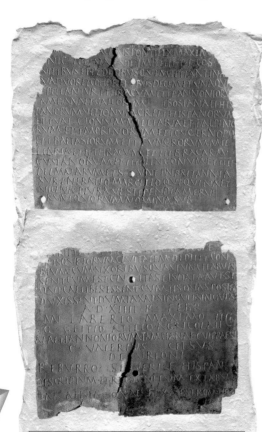

This bronze military diploma from the second century A.D. was issued by the emperor Trajan. It granted a Spanish junior officer Roman citizenship and the right to legal marriage.

ABOUT-FACE!

In A.D. 106, the emperor Trajan conquered Dacia (modern-day Romania) extending the Roman Empire north of its border along the Danube River. Late in his reign (A.D. 98–117), he also defeated the Persians (then ruled by the Parthians), adding Armenia and Mesopotamia to the empire's vast territory. But, for the most part, Rome's expansion stopped with Trajan. His successor, Hadrian (A.D. 117–138), believed that Trajan's empire could not be defended and withdrew from Dacia and Mesopotamia. He then concentrated on strengthening defenses at the Roman frontier. Under Hadrian's rule, the purpose of the Roman army shifted from fighting to build an empire to fighting to keep it.

Roman soldiers were not just skilled fighters; they were also skilled builders. Traveling with them were surveyors, carpenters, stonemasons, engineers, and tile layers. When the soldiers were done fighting, they built new towns and greatly improved existing ones. They added distinctively Roman touches, such as public baths or beautiful arches. The cities they conquered acquired a graceful, Roman look that helped connect them to the empire.

Of all their building projects, the Romans are probably best known for their excellent roads. They built thousands of miles of them, reaching into every corner of the empire. The roads varied according to their location and the materials available. Over marshlands, for example, the Romans built wooden rafts, connected them, and added a layer of gravel on top. Their most beautiful roads were those, like the Via Appia in Rome, that have a surface of five-sided paving slabs perfectly fitted together. Because of their skillful construction, Roman roads could withstand the heavy pounding of soldiers, horses, and carts for hundreds of years. Many ancient Roman roads, or sections of them, are still in use. In addition to ensuring that the empire's army could move around easily, the roads greatly improved trade. They kept the outlying areas of the empire connected to one another and to the more centralized areas. This network of roads, leading in and out of the city of Rome, helped trade thrive throughout the empire. Wealthy Romans got access to the luxuries of far-off places. Markets grew and middle-class merchants prospered.

The Roman army built the empire, but it also had the potential to destroy it. No one was more aware of this power than the emperors. Starting with Octavian, careful rulers watched the military closely for signs of discontent. In addition to allowing their men to keep what they wanted from conquered towns and cities, some emperors added personal gifts. In return, these emperors required deep loyalty and strict discipline from their men.

A COMMON LANGUAGE

The emperors wanted soldiers and Roman officials to live in the lands throughout the empire. This way, the conquered people would be more likely to accept Rome's culture. With the culture, they would accept the Roman language, Latin.

Latin became a unifying element throughout the vast realm, giving very different people a common way to connect.

For a citizen to advance in Roman society, Latin was a requirement. It was the language of government and commerce. The ability to give a good speech was a highly prized art in the world of the Romans. Many people eagerly studied to improve their speaking skills. One favorite source of advice was the book *Orator's Education*. Written by the first-century A.D. author Marcus Fabius Quintilian, this work described the perfect Latin public speaker. He was a man of good morals and education who used logic to persuade his listeners. (Women were not allowed to make speeches in public.)

Quintilian even gave advice on the right gestures to go with a speech. In fact, he described twenty-three different gestures that were sure to win people over. He explained that the one he considered the best "consists of bending the middle finger [of the right hand] against the thumb and extending the other three. . . . If the first finger touches the right-hand edge of the thumbnail with its tip, the other fingers being relaxed, we have a gesture wholly suitable to approval." This gesture is often used by modern-day politicians and other public speakers.

Public speaking was glorified, but gradually, written works became more common. Early Roman history was recorded in Greek. By A.D. 77, Pliny the elder had published the first ten volumes of his *Natural History* in Latin. It developed into an encyclopedia of classical knowledge in 37 volumes. Literature also emerged, particularly in the form of plays. But serious drama had a limited demand. Easily bored, Roman audiences liked action. When a Roman audience shouted, "Bring on the bears!" they meant it. Theater owners competed with each other to give their audiences a spectacle. Wild bears, especially if they were fighting, were always well received. Herds of horses galloping through the theater during intermissions were a sure hit. Some theater owners even arranged for public executions to be carried out in view of the audience.

Men wrote nearly all the books during the period of the Roman Empire, and they wrote only about the wealthy. In spite of public disapproval of female authors, women did produce a few works that were well known in the empire's time. For example, Agrippina the Younger wrote her mother's biography. Hypatia, a Roman-Egyptian expert in astronomy and philosophy, was the first woman to write about mathematics. Only a few letters and poems written by Roman women survive in modern times.

This early second-century tablet is a rare example of a Roman woman's writing in Latin. The woman, who lived in Britain, wrote this birthday invitation to a friend. It was discovered at the Roman fort Vindolanda in Northumberland, Britain.

RELIGION

In a sense, the Romans were very open-minded about religion. This was one reason that the empire, despite its many different cultures, lasted so long. The Romans didn't hesitate to adopt deities from the provinces. For example, they often included the Egyptian goddess, Isis, in their prayers and ceremonies. Roman soldiers were especially devoted to Mithras, a deity that probably came from Persia (modern-day Iran). Greek gods and goddesses were also accepted, especially those representing traits such as loyalty and duty to family and the state. And some Romans believed there was a single god from which all

JEWS IN THE ROMAN EMPIRE

Judaism is an ancient, monotheistic (one-God) religion. Around 1000 B.C., Jews (followers of Judaism) formed the Kingdom of Israel on the eastern banks of the Mediterranean Sea. This kingdom was also known as Judea. The Romans took over Judea in 63 B.C., and Judaism spread throughout the ancient world. The Jews refused to worship the Roman gods and to perform the Romans' religious rituals. As a result, they fought bloody and long revolts against the Romans during the Pax Romana. And although from the time of Antoninus Pius (A.D. 138–161) Jews began to hold jobs at every level of Roman society throughout the empire, they continued to be persecuted at times. This was especially true during the empire's declining years when Romans began to feel that their gods had deserted them. Many Romans felt that their gods were angry because the Jews refused to worship any god but their own.

the other gods and goddesses got their powers. This god was Sol, or the sun god. Sol's believers celebrated his birthday on December 25. Until the empire began having major problems in the third century A.D., the Romans were also fairly accepting of religions, such as Judaism and, later, Christianity, that believed in only one God.

Romans extended their religious faith to their emperors. This belief that the emperor was a god, or at least nearly a god, is sometimes called the emperor cult. Most of the early emperors encouraged this worship from their subjects. All the provinces, cities, and villages set aside at least one day a year for festivities to honor their emperor. The state believed that citizens' devotion to both the gods and the emperor helped keep them united and loyal.

ENTERTAINMENT

Juvenal, the great Roman poet, accused the Romans of letting the emperors keep them quiet with *panem et circenses* (bread and circuses). According to Juvenal, the people didn't care what the emperor was doing, as long as he gave them a good show to watch and bread to eat. To some degree, this was true. The government handed out free food, and the emperors certainly put on good shows. Octavian and later emperors used public money to build places of entertainment. Vespasian, emperor from A.D. 69 to 79, began building the ancient world's greatest amphitheater, or open-air theater: the Colosseum. His son, the emperor Titus, finished it during his reign (A.D. 79–81). More than 50,000 people could watch a performance in the Colosseum.

ROME AT ITS WORST?

Titus staged a great opening for the Roman Colosseum *(below, as the interior looks in the twenty-first century)*. Some scholars believe that, although entertaining, this spectacle was an example of the excess that helped cause the empire's fall. The celebration lasted one hundred days and featured thousands of contests. Ten thousand men fought for their lives—against one another or against wild animals. Nine thousand animals were killed. In its history, more than 200,000 people died in the Colosseum strictly for the entertainment of the Romans.

Because of its 76 entrances and 160 passageways, a full house could be seated within ten minutes.

Romans everywhere in the empire loved the games held at the Colosseum and provincial stadiums. The rich and poor alike eagerly hurried to see gladiators (professional warriors) fight to the death. Gladiators were often from the poorest classes, or they had been taken prisoner and enslaved when the Romans invaded their homelands. They learned most of their fighting tricks in gladiator schools. The Romans greatly admired the strength and courage of the gladiators. After all, these were the traits that built the empire. But the gladiators' chances of surviving a day of games were so low that they performed a death ritual before every event. At the start of the game, they presented themselves before the seats of the emperor and other high officials with these words: "Hail, Caesar! We who are about to die greet thee!"

Probably the oldest form of Roman popular entertainment was chariot racing. The place to go for this was the Circus Maximus. Located in the city of Rome, this racetrack was 680 yards (622 meters) long and 150 yards (137 m) wide. The Romans would build many other racetracks throughout the empire, but none compared to the great Circus Maximus.

Seats at the Circus Maximus were often hard to get, so on race days the line began forming before dawn. There was plenty of standing room, and people could gather on nearby hillsides to watch their favorite team of chariots compete. They knew the races were about to begin when they heard the parade. First came the race officials, followed by musicians. Behind them came the charioteers (drivers) and their horses. Finally came the priests and priestesses for whichever god was being honored at a particular race. Originally, the event was not simply entertainment to the Romans. It was a religious offering to a particular deity.

Chariot racing was a dangerous sport. To keep control of their horses, charioteers often tied the reins around their waist. If the cart tipped, the charioteer could be dragged to his death or crushed by other chariots. Great charioteers positioned their carts to do maximum damage to the other drivers. Causing others to crash was part of the race.

Roman fans took their chariot racing seriously. The following curse on a competitor was found etched into a tablet:

I conjure you up, holy beings and holy names, join in aiding this spell, and
bind . . . strike . . . overturn . . . and break Eucherius, the charioteer . . . tomorrow in the circus at Rome.

WOMEN IN THE GAMES

Even though most Roman women did not lead public lives, a few did compete in the games. Inscriptions, sculptures, mosaics, and writings from ancient Rome indicate that, at times, women competed in gladiatorial events and chariot racing throughout the empire.

In addition to watching games and other performances, all Romans loved spending time at the public baths. Roman bathhouses were located everywhere in the empire and became a privilege expected both by citizens in Rome itself and by provincial subjects. Some of the baths were gifts of the emperors, who wanted to keep average citizens happy and loyal.

The baths were often a three-part experience. First was the tepidarium, where the bather began the bath in room-temperature water. Then came the caladarium, where the bathwater was hot. The bath ended with the cold frigidarium, which invigorated the bather to go out for a stroll through the forum, or local market area. (The forum was the center of any Roman town or city.)

People of all social levels tried to spend at least some time at the baths every day—a habit that made the bathhouses a bit crowded at times. Smaller baths could serve as many as five hundred people, but the big baths could handle as many as 1,500 a day.

THE CONNECTIONS

The Pax Romana would not last forever—nor would the empire itself. However, for hundreds of years, millions of very different people were united under its government, laws, and military. The Romans built roads, bridges, and aqueducts (bridges that carried water) in the towns and cities they conquered, often making them centers of commerce and prosperity. The emperors urged their retiring soldiers and other Romans to settle permanently in the conquered lands.

The result was that the different people of the empire learned and shared the Roman language. The emperors encouraged the worship of traditional gods and of themselves. This common religion also bound the people together. People throughout the empire were united in their love for the Roman spectacles, such as the gladiator matches and chariot races. And in spite of grave social inequalities and the frequent threat of war from within and outside the empire, Romans—rich and poor—were certain that they shared a great destiny. Virgil expressed this belief in *The Aeneid*:

> Romulus [one of the mythic founders of
>   Rome] . . . rejoicing
> takes up the [battles]
> And calls the people after himself
> the Romans
> To these I set no bounds in space
> or time;
> They shall rule forever.

Some historians believe that these connections were the glue that held the Roman Empire together for five hundred years.

CHAPTER TWO

THE SCALES TIP

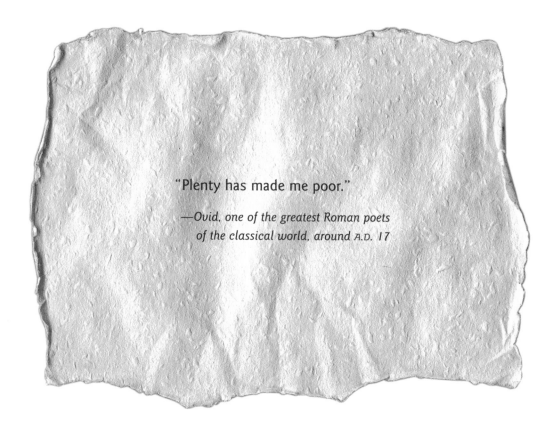

"Plenty has made me poor."

—*Ovid, one of the greatest Roman poets
of the classical world, around* A.D. *17*

During the last years of the Pax Romana, the Roman
Empire was ruled by a series of men known as the Five Good
Emperors. During their reigns, the empire was at its
strongest—both in power and wealth. For some Romans, life
was good.

But even during the reign of the good emperors, there
were some disturbing changes. For example, Antoninus Pius,

SLAVERY

Some residents of the Roman Empire were slaves. After a conquest, Roman military officials were allowed to take prisoners whom they would sell as slaves. Many Roman parents were forced to sell their children as slaves because they could not afford to feed them. Sometimes, selling their children was the only way poor parents could pay off their debts. Later in the empire, this illegal practice became commonplace but was ignored by the government. Although some slaves were treated well, many were beaten, tortured, or even killed by their owners.

who reigned from A.D. 138 to 161, began social changes that further widened the divide between rich and poor. Roman law had once—in word, if not always in practice—protected Roman citizens equally. Now a difference between the wealthy and the poor was written into the law. In courtrooms and legal documents, the rich were referred to as *honestiores* or *potentiores*, and the poor as *humiliores*. Once these labels were in place, sentences for crimes were decided by social category, instead of citizenship. For instance, the crime of moving boundary markers—that is, stealing a neighbor's land—carried different sentences. The rich were forced to leave the empire. But the poor were beaten or imprisoned.

By the time Marcus Aurelius, the last of the Five Good Emperors, died in A.D. 180, the connections that had once held the empire together began to fail. The security of being

This Roman bronze statue of Marcus Aurelius is from the second century A.D.

Roman would soon be lost. Marcus Aurelius spent years on the battlefield fighting back the barbarians on the northern frontier and the Persians in the east. Although it took him most of his reign to do it, he made the empire's borders safe. But when he died, the barbarians quickly renewed their siege. Also during the reign of Marcus Aurelius, a terrible disease swept through the Roman Empire. Known as the Antonine Plague, it killed one-third of the empire's population. The dead included large numbers of soldiers.

Some historians think that Aurelius himself was one of the plague's victims. In the words of the historian Dio Cassius, the empire seemed suddenly to have "plunged [from a kingdom of gold into] a kingdom of . . . iron and rust."

Aurelius left power in the hands of his nineteen-year-old son, Commodus, who had his own ideas about running an

COMMODUS

Commodus had a taste for blood. He loved gladiator combat and brought it to a new level of cruelty when he placed people with disabilities in the arena and forced them to fight each other. He would then step into the arena himself and kill them. He also fought battles against gladiators in the Colosseum and always won. Whether the fact that he was the emperor guaranteed his victories isn't clear.

Most modern scholars believe that Commodus's behavior indicates a progressive mental illness. He took to dressing like the hero and part-god Hercules. Like Hercules, he carried a club wherever he went. He also renamed everything in sight after himself. For example, the city of Rome became Colonia Lucia Annia Commodiana. The legions became Commodianae and the Senate became the Commodian Fortunate Senate. The people were referred to as Commodianus. He even renamed the months of the Roman calendar with his various titles.

empire. To keep warring tribes quiet, he allowed them to settle on Roman land. He then marched home to the city of Rome in victory. At first, the poor and the soldiers liked Commodus. He was very generous, giving them money and other gifts. To fund the gifts he gave, he simply taxed the wealthy, including members of the Senate. This was a dangerous move. He was assassinated in A.D. 192, as he was bathing.

THE SEVERANS

When the Roman people heard that Commodus had been murdered, they hoped for a peaceful transfer of power and a return to prosperity and justice. Instead, the government was once again thrown into chaos. The Pax Romana was truly over. Enemies were pounding at the empire's borders, the population had already been hit by plague, and the economy was failing. The high toll from the plague meant there were fewer taxpayers and less revenue available to the state. There was also lowered agricultural output, creating food shortages and higher prices.

Septimius Severus grabbed the throne in A.D. 193. Severus was not Roman by birth. He was originally from northern Africa, a sign of Rome's increasing reliance on the provinces and their growing influence. The African provinces, for instance, had become the main source of the empire's olive oil and grain.

A respected general, Severus pushed back the foreign invaders and got the army under control. He began what was known as the Severan Dynasty, a series of soldier-emperors. He also led a successful campaign against the empire's neighbor, Persia. This powerful eastern empire had a long history of war with the Romans. Severus marched home from Persia in triumph, ensuring the future of his dynasty. His conquest brought Rome enough gold and silver to temporarily steady its economy.

Knowing how dependent he was on the army, Severus was good to his soldiers. He not only raised their pay, but he also let them marry and live with their families in the villages and towns of the empire. He also increased their numbers.

Severus paid the bills by placing the economy that he had steadied under renewed pressure. To temporarily strengthen it, he lowered the value of Roman coins by decreasing their gold and silver content. This was meant to increase export sales, since foreign money could then buy Roman goods more cheaply than Roman money could. The amount of foreign money would grow in the empire's economy. Because foreign goods would be more expensive to Romans, it would also decrease imports, keeping more of their own money within the economy. This meant that Severus could raise taxes further, and give more bonuses to his soldiers. When he was dying, he gave his sons the following advice: ". . . live in harmony [with each other], enrich the soldiers, and scorn all others."

Although his sons and their successors ignored Severus's advice on living in harmony, they did enrich the army. They did this by taxing citizens of the city of Rome at the same high levels as people in the provinces. This did not sit well with Rome's residents, since they had always enjoyed lower taxes or complete exemption from taxes. Caraculla Severan, who ruled from A.D. 211 to 217, was

This painting on wood from Egypt shows the emperor Septimius Severus (upper right) and his family, Julia Domna (upper left), Caracalla (lower right) and Geta (lower left), whose face is obscured.

especially hard on the people of Rome. Dio Cassius described life under Caraculla:

> [Caraculla] took pains to strip, despoil, and grind down all the rest of mankind, and not the least the senators. . . . [P]rovisions . . . were exacted of us in great quantities and from every side, sometimes without payment, sometimes with additional cost to

ourselves—all of which he either bestowed upon the soldiers or sold at retail; and there were the gifts which he kept demanding of wealthy private persons and from communities; and the taxes. . . . [W]e were also compelled to build at our own expense all sorts of houses for him.

In A.D. 212, Caraculla granted citizenship to all free men throughout the provinces. He did it to win friends, but also to gain taxpayers. His action had a big effect on the empire. Italian Rome was fading, and a more universal Rome was appearing. The benefits of being a Roman citizen were being spread to more people, but the benefits were decreasing sharply.

LOSING GROUND

By the early third century A.D., Romans in the Senate were outnumbered by non-Romans. Many of the best government jobs were held by former military men from the provinces. Even emperors, like Septimius Severus, came from provincial lands. Macrinus (A.D. 217–218), another non-Roman emperor, had not even been a senator, a first in the empire's history.

The power of outsiders was growing, and the power of native Romans was not. This was clear in the army. The emperors had long allowed foreigners to serve as their auxiliary forces. By the end of the second century, these outsiders filled the legions. They even reached into the heart of the army, the Praetorian Guards.

The new emperors gave the soldiers much more freedom than earlier emperors had. Some historians believe that the emperors relaxed the rules because many of the foreign troops would not abide by the old rules. The looser rules weakened discipline and military response time. Soldiers who lived away from their camps took longer to get to defensive positions. Also, because they lived at home, soldiers could serve many years with the same people and often the same commander. This made them more loyal to their own leader and unit than to the empire. Some soldiers had no loyalties at all.

The army changed in other ways, as well. Non-Roman emperors often had no ties to the city of Rome. They set up their base of operations in cities where they were more at home and closer to the points along the borders most likely to be attacked. This shift meant that Rome was no longer the working center of the empire, which further reduced its influence over the realm.

The Severans did not profit from their generosity to the army. Of the seven rulers in the dynasty, only Septimius Severus died of natural causes while still in power. The others were either forced out or murdered by their armies. When the last of the Severans was murdered in A.D. 235, chaos ensued. Aurelius Victor, biographer of the emperors, described it this way: "Armies became a law unto themselves, terrorizing the population, [making] and [breaking] emperors at will."

For nearly fifty years, between A.D. 235 and 284, one faction or another of the army chose who was in power at any given time. Soldiers could and did put their own leaders on the throne. Or they could—and often did—murder their emperor in his sleep. Other emperors died in battle, either against outside attackers or other Romans struggling for power. These deaths kept the empire in a nearly constant state of turmoil.

Military leaders feared their own troops' power and often had little control over them. Some soldiers threatened the people, stealing their money or property. Others forced citizens to house and feed them. Sometimes villagers fled their homes in terror. The following is a plea for help from the people of the province of Thrace. They sent it to Gordian III, who ruled the empire from A.D. 238 to 244.

> During the most fortunate . . . time of your reign you have often stated . . . that the villages should be . . . improved instead of having the inhabitants driven from their homes. . . . We . . . [pray] that you may graciously grant our petition to this effect. . . .
>
> In the past as long as [we] remained undisturbed and unharmed, [we] paid [our] tribute. . . . But when [they] . . . proceed[ed] to [treat us harshly] and employ violence . . . [our] village began to decline.
>
> [The] soldiers . . . leave their proper routes and come to us, and . . . compel us to provide them with hospitality and supplies and pay us no money.

The days when every soldier feared and honored his emperor were gone.

HARD TIMES

To get the cash to fight one another, defend the borders, and keep their troops from murdering them, the emperors continued to lower the amount of gold and silver in coins until Roman money became almost worthless. This caused goods produced within the empire to rise in price just to cover the cost to produce them. People living within the Roman economy paid more for necessities, even though their incomes didn't rise.

This economic pressure is known as inflation. Inflation was especially hard on Romans living in the western portion of the empire. They did not have the active trade or vast agricultural resources of the eastern and North African provinces. As a result, these Romans often stopped using money to buy goods. Instead, they traded goods and services among themselves. This is called bartering. Even the government traded goods in exchange for tax money.

Government costs remained huge and continued to grow. By the third century, the empire spent half of its total budget on an army that failed to do its job. This failure led to another expense—bribes paid to the barbarian tribes not to cross the empire's borders. Once they got the money, the barbarians continued to cross wherever they could. As early as Caraculla's reign at the start of the third century, Rome was already paying as much in bribes as it was paying its own army.

Clearly, the government was not using its money well. But most Roman citizens didn't worry much at first. They may have even liked seeing the rich pay high taxes, for instance. But rebellion rose throughout the empire when the emperors began raiding public funds. This money paid for free grain and entertainment After all, by the third and fourth centuries, Roman citizens had 175 holidays out of

365 days in the year. They needed something to do during their holidays.

Not everyone got caught in the money squeeze. Some of the richest Romans grew even richer. They made fortunes by lending money at high interest rates to the provinces. The provinces were forced to pay the high interest so they could pay their taxes or tribute to the emperors.

There was another worry for Roman citizens besides the military and the economy. They could no longer expect

THE SILK ROAD

Some Romans blamed the rich for their money problems. They believed that the wealthy spent too much on luxuries bought along the Silk Road. This series of roads and trails connected the Roman Empire with empires to the east. Luxury items were not the only things that traveled this route. Religions like Buddhism and Christianity, new ideas, books, languages, and disease spread by the Silk Road as well.

Romans who had the cash eagerly bought spices, beautiful textiles, jewelry, and other expensive goods from Persia, India, and China. The trade was good for Roman provincial cities along the Silk Road. Cities like Palmyra (in Syria) and Alexandria (in Egypt) grew very rich from the trade. But some Romans believed that the gold coins spent by their citizens in other empires weakened the economy at home.

protection from crimes committed against them. For example, their own soldiers freely entered citizens' homes and demanded money. And if they went to court, they could not expect a fair decision. The historian Herodian summarized the injustice of the time:

> Any person even summoned to court by an informer was immediately found guilty and went away from the proceedings stripped of his entire property. Every day one could see the wealthy of yesterday reduced to beggary for the future. . . . The pretext was always the constant need of supplies for the soldiers.

THREATS FROM WITHOUT AND WITHIN

The German tribes had long been a threat to the Roman Empire. Romans had not forgotten the terrible defeat they had suffered in A.D. 9 in the Teutoburg Forest. But by 230, a different group of Germanic people from Scandinavia had arrived. They were known as the Goths. Within ten years, the Goths became Rome's biggest threat from outside its borders. In the 240s, the Goths began a series of attacks on the empire's eastern provinces. In 251, they won a battle against the Romans in which they killed the emperor Decius. They then began attacks by sea on Asia Minor, an area that is now Turkey. Other Germanic tribes, including the Franks and Alamanni, attacked Gaul (modern-day France), one of the empire's major agricultural areas. Some of these invaders pushed as far south as Spain.

This detail of a monumental marble sarcophagus (tomb) depicts a battle between the Romans and the Goths in approximately A.D. 250.

At the same time, the Persians began an organized and deadly assault on the empire. In 260, they attacked the eastern frontier and captured the Roman emperor Valerian.

In addition to the outside threats, the empire suffered new internal power struggles. Seeing the empire's weakness, some provinces formed their own governments. In the west, Gaul, Great Britain, and Spain broke away and became (from 260 to 273) the independent Gallic Empire. From 286 to 296, Britain formed its own independent state. The Italy-centered Roman Empire could not stop them.

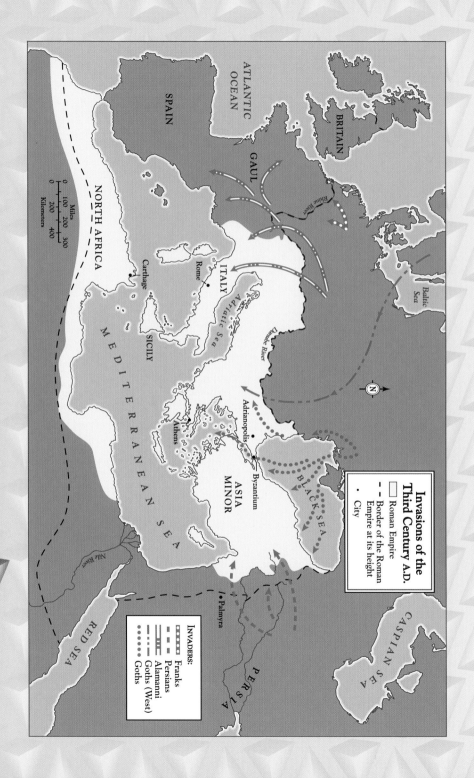

Invasions of the Third Century A.D.

Roman Empire

– – Border of the Roman Empire at its height

• City

INVADERS:

Franks

Persians

Alamanni

Goths (West)

Goths

ATLANTIC OCEAN

SPAIN

BRITAIN

GAUL

Rhine River

NORTH AFRICA

Carthage

Rome

ITALY

Adriatic Sea

SICILY

Baltic Sea

Danube River

M E D I T E R R A N E A N   S E A

Adrianopolis

Athens

Byzantium

ASIA MINOR

BLACK SEA

Miles

0
100
200   Kilometers
300
400

NILE River

RED SEA

Palmyra

PERSIA

CASPIAN SEA

N

QUEEN ZENOBIA

After their invasion on Rome's eastern border, the Persians were pushed back by the Romans, with the help of the city of Palmyra. Located in what is now Syria, this wealthy city-state was ruled by Queen Zenobia. But in 270 to 272, Zenobia invaded Rome's richest eastern provinces, including Egypt. She rode into battle with her men. Zenobia claimed to be descended from Cleopatra, the famous and ambitious queen of Egypt, who was once considered an enemy of Rome. Zenobia planned to build her own empire and declared herself Augusta. But the Romans defeated her and her army. Historians are unclear on what happened next. Some think she died after the Romans captured her. Others think that she was taken back to Rome, where she became a celebrity among the rich.

Roman government—and its laws—no longer protected the common citizen as they had in the earlier days of the empire. The once proud and disciplined military had become a public menace. Taxes were rising, the value of money was dropping, and the gap between the poor and the rich was getting wider. Trade and commerce were breaking down. But even greater dangers were at Rome's borders, where outsiders pushed to get in.

CHAPTER THREE
THE WARRING TRIBES

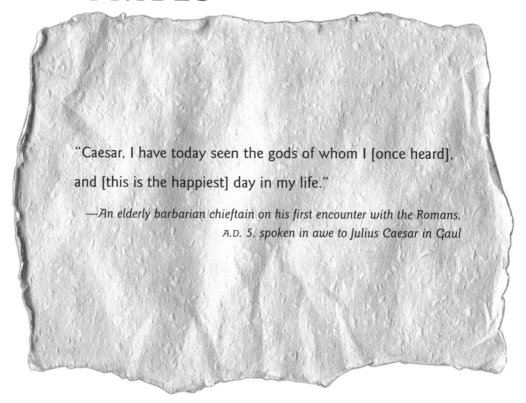

"Caesar, I have today seen the gods of whom I [once heard],
and [this is the happiest] day in my life."

—*An elderly barbarian chieftain on his first encounter with the Romans,*
A.D. 5, spoken in awe to Julius Caesar in Gaul

Just who were the people threatening Rome from its
borderlands? The Greeks and Romans called them
barbarians. Originally, the term described someone who
couldn't speak or write Greek. Later, the Romans added
another meaning: barbarians were those who were a threat
to Greek and Roman civilization.

The barbarians lived throughout the lands to the north

and northeast of the Roman Empire. As early as 390 B.C., Celtic tribes thundered down the Alps (a mountain range in Europe) to challenge the Roman Republic. The Romans called these tribes Gauls, and their homeland, Gaul.

The Celts boldly attacked the republic at its center, burning the city of Rome to the ground. They left only after Rome paid them a huge ransom. Then they settled in what is now Europe, west of the Rhine River. In response to the Celts' victory, the Romans began to better organize and train their military.

CELTS AND GAULS

Historians disagree about whether all Gauls were Celtic. Many people think that the Celts were made up of subgroups that spanned the entire European continent and beyond. The first to categorize the Celts was Julius Caesar, who waged war on them in the first century b.c. (but called them Gauls). Caesar broke them into three groups, according to their general location in what is now known as Europe: the Belgae (northern Europe), Celts (central), and the Aquitani (southwest). To confuse things further, historians now think the Belgae were actually Celts who had joined Germanic groups. The Celts who fought Caesar, and who later became subjects of the Roman Empire, grew to be so much like the Romans that other barbarian tribes would sometimes attack them, believing them to be Romans.

A Roman statue of Julius Caesar from the first century B.C.

By the 200s B.C., the Roman army was strong enough to defeat the Celts and take part of their land. Julius Caesar took the rest of it for the empire 150 years later.

The Celts may have been pushed toward Rome by other Germanic tribes, which had settled further east and north of them hundreds of years earlier. These newcomers, who all spoke a language similar to modern German, came from Scandinavia and Denmark. Many historians believe that they left their homelands due to hunger and poverty. They included the Goths, Alamanni, Burgundians, Franks, and Vandals. The Goths and Vandals migrated eastward toward the Black Sea. Others went south along the Rhine and Danube rivers.

The Romans and Greeks regarded the barbarians as subhuman, unwashed, unread, and brutal. But they readily bought their slaves and recruited their men as auxiliaries to the Roman army.

The Greek historian and geographer Strabo wrote that it was the choice of these warring people to live in poverty, violence, and ignorance. He found their behavior abnormal and cruel. For example, he reported that, rather than be captured by their enemies, they killed themselves and their children. The men threw themselves into the campfires and the mothers murdered their babies. His descriptions of the tribes were grim:

> [They are known for] suspending the heads of their enemies from their horses' necks on their return from battle, and when they arrived, nailing [these heads] to their gates.

The tribes may have been violent, but Strabo clearly admired their warrior skills.

> [They are] . . . furnished with light arms for the purposes of robbery. . . . [Their cavalry have] trained their horses to sink down to their knees, in case of necessity. [Their horses] are superior to all other breeds, both in fleetness and ease of [riding].

DAILY LIFE

Ties of blood and loyalty defined all aspects of tribal living. Most tribes operated on a system known to the Romans as *comitatus*. Their ties to family and fellow tribespersons defined who the people were and what was expected of them. The ties were important not only in battle, but in day-to-day living. Even the tribe's economy was based on rewards for a duty fulfilled. The ties of family brought about many disputes, both among tribal members and between distinct tribes. It was the duty of family members to avenge the death or injury of relatives, regardless of whether the attacker was a member of their own tribe or another tribe.

In general, the tribal groups had no formal government. But they did have laws. For some crimes, the people could be punished by drowning or hanging. Women were not always treated fairly, and were usually sold into marriage. They were also held to a higher standard of morality than men. If a woman was unfaithful to her husband, for example, she could be killed and her body thrown into a peat bog. In some groups, the people chose judges to serve as leaders in times of crisis. Some tribes elected chieftains, some of whom were female. Many of the tribal people along Rome's borders were nomadic (moving from place to place). Others, such as the Celts and some Goths,

This detail from a terra-cotta frieze shows a Celtic woman in battle. It is from an Italian frieze of the second century B.C.

48

CELTIC AND GERMANIC LANGUAGES

One difference between the Celts and Germanic peoples is their language. Although Celtic (or Gaulist) and Germanic languages have some related words, they are separate subgroups of Indo-European languages. The Celtic and Germanic cultures are very old, and there are many gaps in our knowledge of their early history and the development of their languages. The earliest writings of the Celts come from the sixth century B.C. The Germans' come from the second century A.D.

lived in communities. Barbarian settlements were generally loose clusters of houses that had no town center. This was quite different from Roman towns, with their forums and public buildings. According to Julius Caesar's firsthand account in *The Gallic Wars*, land in many barbarian settlements could be claimed by the entire group, rather than by individuals.

The Goths' houses were often long structures with central aisles that led to separate chambers. Families lived at one end of the house, and their livestock were kept at the other end. Some houses, like those of the Celts, were round structures made of wood with thatch roofs. Dwellings such as these made the Roman villas look very sophisticated.

From excavations of their dwellings and burial sites, we know that these tribal groups made and used simple tools, such as the plow. They made pottery, some with designs stamped across the surface. They also made many weapons, including swords and lances. Experts have also found wooden furniture with carved designs. As early as 500 B.C., the Celts developed a style of design known as La Tène. La Tène uses patterns of woven curves and spirals, which are also seen in Celtic manuscripts and stone crosses from the Middle Ages (around A.D. 500s to 1500s). Many of the tribes were farmers, although some grew only enough crops to feed their families. Their diets were very simple, mostly consisting of grains, seeds, milk, and fruit. They hunted some game, especially waterfowl. Some grew beans and peas. Salt was always in demand.

For entertainment, most of these tribal people, like the Romans, enjoyed competitions in strength and endurance. They loved gambling. Young men performed spear or sword dances, often naked. Tribal people liked music, and played different types

This terra-cotta vase from between the third and first centuries B.C. is an example of the Celtic style called La Tène.

GREATER THAN MONEY

Salt was highly prized in the ancient and medieval worlds. People used it to preserve their foods. Roman soldiers were sometimes paid in salt. (The modern English word "salary" is based on the Latin word *sal*, which means "salt.") The Romans controlled the price of salt throughout the days of the empire. They raised the price if they needed money for their wars and lowered it when they were at peace. The Germanic tribes traded slaves to buy salt from caravans that came all the way from the Sahara Desert in northern Africa.

of fifes (similar to flutes) and lyres (similar to harps). They also performed songs and told sagas (long, detailed stories) by their campfires.

WAGING WAR

The barbarians were known as fierce fighters. They took a different approach to battle than the Romans. For example, some warriors looked terrifying before battle. The tribal men often fought naked or covered in animal skins. Some northern tribes painted their bodies blue and wore their hair in knots or braids, or stiffened into spikes. Most warriors either moaned or screeched as they attacked. They used this tactic, as well as the element of surprise, to gain an advantage over their enemies.

ANCIENT EVIDENCE

Historians know what tribal people ate because scientists have examined the entrails (bowels) of well-preserved bodies found in the peat bogs of what was once the northern Roman Empire (modern-day Great Britain). The bodies also give clues about what the people looked like. They were taller than the Romans, who reported that the Celts were giants. They were probably heavily muscled. Their clothing was so well woven that it was popular even among the Romans. Many members of these tribes wore ornamental brooches, or clasps, to fasten their cloaks, and some wore fancy combs in their hair.

Archaeologists have found many weapons and other instruments of war in their excavations (on-site studies of the remains of a civilization) of tribal settlements. Some of their battle gear, such as swords, lances, helmets, and shields, had complex designs, precious metals, and even jewels worked into them. This is especially true of those found in Celtic societies.

Many of these groups worshipped gods of war. The greatest Gothic war god was Tiwaz, who guarded the community and granted it law and order. Late in the Roman period, Woden emerged as another war god. The Roman soldiers feared the barbarians because they were said to mutilate the bodies of their fallen enemies or take captives as sacrifices (gifts) to these war gods. Warrior priestesses would sometimes hang prisoners upside down, slit their throats, and let the blood drip into large bronze bowls. Then they used the blood in their ceremonies.

A MIX OF LANGUAGES

Most barbarians spoke various types of German. The Celts had their own ancient language. The Germanic and Celtic tribes at times lived in the same places and borrowed words from one another. This kind of transfer from language to language produced many of the modern European languages, including English. Although English is made up of mostly Latin and German words, it uses some Celtic words as well. For example, "bucket," "car," "noggin," and "flannel" are all taken from the Celtic language.

A few of the barbarian peoples used a simple alphabet to carve on wood or stone. The alphabet was made up of characters called runes, a

This rune stone from the seventh century A.D. was found in Sweden. The runic lettering is supplemented with a carving of a warrior.

ENGLISH WORDS TAKEN FROM LATIN AND GERMAN:

The majority of English words come from two languages: Latin and German. Words taken from these two older languages each make up nearly half of the English vocabulary. Here are a few examples:

FROM LATIN:	FROM GERMAN:
Soldiers	Clock
Navy	Kindergarten
Maximum	Rocket
Pectoral muscle	Hamburger

Germanic word meaning "secret." Most people did not know how to read the runes, each of which represented a sound from German. The earliest runic writings were probably the work of priests who were casting spells or creating charms. They carved the characters onto the surface of jewelry, coins, wood, or stone. Runes from the second century A.D. were simple characters made with straight lines so they could be carved easily. Later runes were more complex. Archaeologists have found at least four thousand examples of runic writings, which could consist of a single character or a series of characters. When the warring tribes became Christian, the church taught them the Latin alphabet and the runes fell out of use.

Despite their differences, the warring tribes had one thing in common: their envy of the Roman Empire. To them, the Romans were godlike. The tribes admired the Romans' advanced culture and great wealth. Even the most feared barbarians of all, the Huns, later marveled at what the Romans had built. One Hun khan (leader) summed up the barbarian point of view when he told the Roman emperor Justinian, "In your empire . . . there is a superabundance of everything—including . . . the impossible."

Their admiration for the Romans did not stop the barbarians from making savage attacks on the empire, however. By the end of the third century A.D., many different tribes were spread out along the length of the empire's borders, waiting.

CHAPTER FOUR

SPLENDOR AND DIVISION

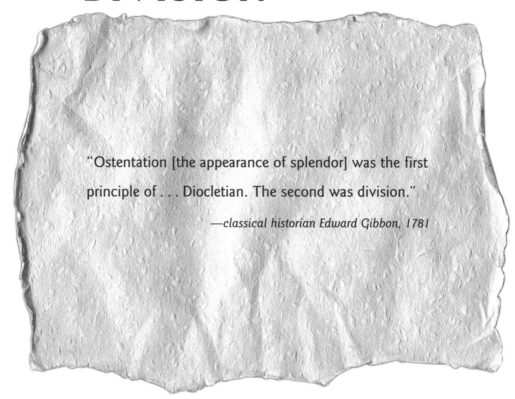

"Ostentation [the appearance of splendor] was the first

principle of . . . Diocletian. The second was division."

—*classical historian Edward Gibbon, 1781*

D iocletian knew what he was facing when he became
emperor in A.D. 284. In the third century, only one of more
than twenty emperors had died of natural causes. Most had
died on the battlefields or had been murdered. All of the
empire's boundaries were at risk. The empire was going broke.
There was chaos in the streets and in the army. Diocletian
knew that by becoming emperor, he was putting his life on

the line. But Diocletian beat the odds. He ruled from 284 to 305 and stepped down on his own, a first for an emperor.

Like some of his fellow emperors, Diocletian was from the province of Illyria, on the eastern coast of the Adriatic Sea. Possibly the son of a freed slave, he worked his way up in the Roman army to the rank of general. He was known for his skill at solving problems and organizing people.

Diocletian immediately saw that the empire was too big for one man to handle alone. He found a way to divide the provinces so they could be better managed.

This Roman bust of the emperor Diocletian has been preserved since the third century A.D.

THE TETRARCHY

First, in 286, Diocletian split the empire into two parts: the eastern and the western. He put a fellow army officer, Maximian, in charge of the western part of the empire. Maximian would be based in Milan, Italy, 300 miles (483 kilometers) from the traditional capital city of Rome.

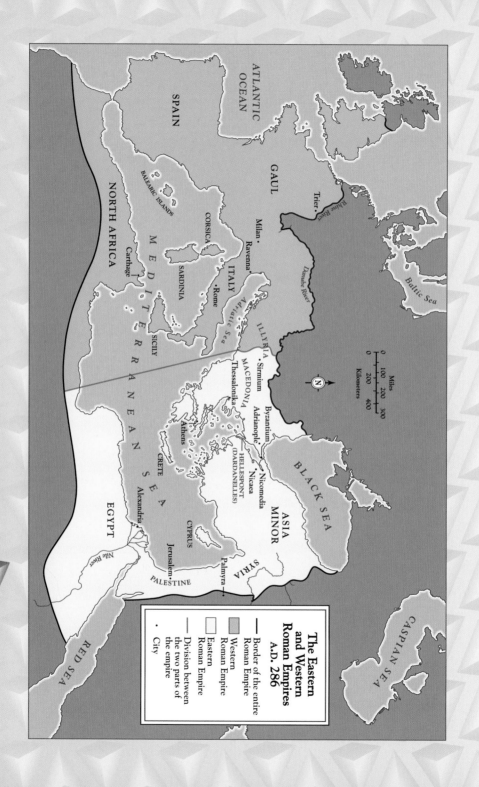

The Eastern and Western Roman Empires
A.D. 286

— Border of the entire Roman Empire

☐ Western Roman Empire

☐ Eastern Roman Empire

— Division between the two parts of the empire

• City

ATLANTIC OCEAN

SPAIN

GAUL

NORTH AFRICA

BALEARIC ISLANDS

CORSICA

Milan •
Ravenna •

SARDINIA

Carthage •

ITALY

• Rome

M E D I T E R R A N E A N   S E A

SICILY

Adriatic Sea

ILLYRIA

Sirmium •
Adrianople •

MACEDONIA

Thessalonika •

Athens •

CRETE

Byzantium •

Nicomedia •
Nicaea •

HELLESPONT (DARDANELLES)

CYPRUS

Jerusalem •
PALESTINE

Palmyra •

SYRIA

ASIA MINOR

BLACK SEA

EGYPT

Alexandria •

Nile River

RED SEA

Trier •

Rhine River

Danube River

Baltic Sea

CASPIAN SEA

N

Miles
0   100   200   300
0   200   400
Kilometers

THE RALLY

Two emperors preceding Diocletian helped prevent Rome's collapse in the third century. Claudius II (who ruled from A.D. 268 to 270) was commander of the Roman army when they defeated the Goths at the Battle of Naissus in 268. His victory was so decisive that he became known as "Gothicus." He died in 270, possibly from smallpox. Aurelianus (who ruled from A.D. 270 to 275) was a Roman cavalry commander at Naissus and led the battle against Queen Zenobia in A.D. 272. The successful campaigns of these two men restored the empire's lost territory in both the East and the West. Both emperors were foreign-born. Aurelianus was from the province of Dacia, and Claudius had come from a barbarian tribe.

Diocletian took over the eastern part and based himself in the city of Nicomedia, in present-day Turkey. Next, Diocletian appointed two junior emperors to help the senior emperors. The juniors would take over when it was time for replacements. That way, there would be no fighting over power when an emperor needed to be replaced.

Additionally, the two junior emperors would be experienced at governing when they took over from the emperor. This four-man team of two senior emperors and two junior emperors was called a tetrarchy. The historian Aurelius Victor in his *Lives of the Emperors* explained how the plan would work:

[Diocletian made] a sort of division of the Empire: . . . all the countries beyond the Gallic Alps were entrusted to Constantius [as junior to Maximian]; Maximian looked after Africa and Italy; Galerius [junior to Diocletian] Illyria as far as the Black Sea; and Diocletian retained all the rest.

Later, Diocletian divided each of the two halves of the empire into six sections. In turn, he divided these sections into a total of one hundred subsections. Then he appointed an official to govern each of these subsections. He believed that smaller areas of territory would be easier to manage. They would also prevent the officials in charge from gaining too much power.

Of course, not everyone liked Diocletian or his changes. The writer Lacantius related a fellow Christian's thoughts on the changes:

THE PROBLEM OF SUCCESSION

Diocletian's plan to have a set way to pass power from one emperor to the next (known as succession) was a good one. The fact that the empire lacked a succession policy had in the past led to civil wars when an emperor died. Diocletian's plan was meant to prevent these costly battles for power among the military leaders.

While Diocletian . . . was ruining everything, he could not keep his hands even from god. This man, through avarice [greed] and cowardice, overturned the world. For he made three men sharers of his rule; the world was divided into four parts, and the armies were multiplied. . . . The number of those receiving [pay from the state] was so much larger than the number of those paying [taxes] that because of the enormous size of the assessments, the resources of the tenant farmer were exhausted, fields were abandoned, and cultivated areas were transformed into wilderness.

For the twenty years of his reign, Diocletian held the tetrarchy together. But he was constantly worried that someone would break it up. For this reason, he tried to destroy all rivals—real or imagined. He was obsessed with the loyalty of his soldiers and keeping back the barbarians from the borders. He believed that to be taken seriously and be obeyed, he had to stand apart from the citizens.

MILITARY REFORMS

Diocletian made some big changes in the military. To begin with, he increased its size by about one-third. This was almost certainly in response to the strengthening power of the Sassanids along the eastern frontier. Wisely, he considered them a threat to the Roman Empire.

Just how many Roman soldiers there were in the late empire is greatly debated. One estimate often cited is

435,266 men during Diocletian's rule, expanding to as many as 600,000 after his reign.

The army's legionaries and auxiliaries were transformed into *limitanei*, or frontier garrisons, and *comitatenses*, mobile field units. The frontier soldiers were placed at hotspots along the three important borders: the Rhine and Danube rivers and the eastern frontier. These points were heavily fortified. Where necessary, Diocletian built new forts with stone walls more than 10 feet (3 meters) thick. Towers rising above the walls provided lookouts and platforms. From these, Roman soldiers had an advantage over any advancing enemy troops. From above, the Romans could shoot arrows or spears at their attackers or scald them with hot liquids. Heavily armed soldiers guarded the gates. Diocletian's walls were designed to protect his men until the mobile field reinforcements arrived. In all, 4,000 miles (6,437 km) of the empire's borders were strengthened.

Each frontier unit probably consisted of fewer than one thousand infantrymen. Each mobile cavalry unit had some five hundred men. Sometimes foot soldiers and cavalry fought alongside one another. The goal was to have highly mobile troops that could find and strike invaders fast. In fact, the infantry was often more mobile than the cavalry, since they didn't need food or water for their horses.

Diocletian had two purposes in reforming the military. One was to break the army into smaller units so they could respond to invasions on the borders more quickly. And the other was to limit the power of the generals.

Some historians believe that Diocletian's reforms greatly weakened the army. They accuse him of paying too much attention to the borders and too little to the training, arms, and morale of the traditional legionaries. Critics also say that he hired too many barbarians and other foreign soldiers. Some of these auxiliaries proved disloyal to the empire.

ECONOMIC REFORMS

Diocletian also made economic reforms. By this time, Roman coins were almost worthless. For example, "silver" coins were copper dipped in a thin glaze of silver. Diocletian tried to stop the decline in the value of money by returning to a set amount of gold in the empire's coins. But this idea didn't work. The empire no longer had enough gold to put into the coins.

To make taxes easier to collect, Diocletian tried to streamline the process. He returned to a simple, two-tax system: property taxes and personal taxes. But to cover his military reforms, he had to set the rates of these taxes very high. Diocletian made enemies when he required everyone to pay taxes. He made only one exception: members of the Roman Senate and their descendants. These Romans got back their tax-free status, which they'd lost during the previous century. Exemption from paying taxes took a heavy burden off the richest members of Roman society and moved it to the poor and middle class. The burden made some farmers, merchants, and traders give up hope, abandon their workplaces, and join roaming gangs that took what they

THE TAX BURDEN

Not only did the middle class have to pay very high taxes, but individuals from each community were also held responsible for collecting the taxes. If they didn't collect what the empire expected, they had to supply the difference from their own funds.

needed from frightened citizens.

To further simplify the tax system and ensure a regular flow of cash each year, Diocletian decreed that Romans had to remain in their professions—forever. In addition, they were no longer free to move throughout the empire. These measures extended to their children, as well. This made it easier to keep track of taxpayers and allowed the empire to keep its tax income at the expected totals.

Rome's middle class soon understood the brutal truth. If they couldn't pay the taxes, they—and maybe their families—would go to prison or be sold as slaves. As a result, many people handed over their property to the nearest big estate. The estate paid their taxes, and the farmers went on working the same land as *colonii*, or tenants.

In A.D. 301, Diocletian made one more economic reform in an attempt to stop inflation. He froze prices and wages at a level he decided was fair. He sent out a notice to the people. Known as Diocletian's Price Edict, it listed what the people could pay for goods and services. If citizens did not use his price guidelines, they would be executed.

RELIGIOUS REFORMS

For many people throughout the empire, the one bright spot during the difficult third century was hope offered by new religions, coming mostly from the East. For example, Christianity offered the promise of life after death. The idea of heavenly rewards was especially appealing to the poor. The churches were run first by apostles (leaders), and later by their students, the bishops. The bishops, in turn, were helped by the priests in spreading the teachings of Jesus. These teachings became very popular.

Nobody knows for sure how many Christians lived in the empire by the time Diocletian took over. But it is known that by A.D. 300 they had a lot of influence and property. The Romans who still practiced the empire's

JUPITER   PLUTON   PERSEPHONE   NEPTUNUS   AMPHITRITE

The Romans' pagan religion worshipped many gods. Among them were those shown in this relief: (from left) Jupiter, Pluto, Persephone, Neptune, and Aphrodite.

official pagan religion began to take notice. Believing that their gods demanded respect and tribute, they wondered if the Christians could be the cause of the empire's many problems. Maybe the gods and goddesses were angry.

Searching for ways to strengthen Roman unity, Diocletian demanded that the people return to their traditional pagan religion. This old religion centered on the many gods and goddesses of the ancient world. But,

CHRISTIANITY IN ANCIENT ROME

Christianity is a monotheistic (one god) religion that was practiced by a growing number of people in the Roman world. Some Jews became followers of the influential teacher Jesus of Nazareth. After Jesus was crucified, followers who believed he had risen from the dead formed an offshoot of Judaism called Christianity. Like Judaism, it recognized only one God. However, it defined three aspects of the deity—Father, Son, and Holy Spirit—called the Trinity. Jesus's teachings also stressed human equality, which was particularly appealing to the poor. Finally, the inspiring examples of the martyrs (people who died for their religion) made Christianity an attractive alternative to polytheistic (many god) religions. The Christian Bible is a collection of both Judaic (Old Testament) and Christian (New Testament) writings. In the third century, Christianity began to spread wherever the Roman roads went.

from the time of Octavian, it also extended to the emperors. Romans had always believed that their civilization was favored by the gods. The emperor was a sort of human god who directed the worldly affairs of the favored empire. To encourage this renewed faith in the state and emperor, Diocletian began to dress like a god and insisted on being addressed like one. For example, he liked to be called "Lord and Master." Aurelius Victor described him as follows:

> [Diocletian . . . wore] a cloak embroidered in gold and [coveted] shoes of silk and purple decorated with a great many gems. Though this went beyond what befitted a citizen and was characteristic of an arrogant and lavish spirit, it was nevertheless of small consequence in comparison with the rest. Indeed he . . . [allowed] himself to be publicly called lord and to be named god. . . .

To the dismay of many Christian and non-Christian Romans alike, Diocletian also demanded that they worship him as their personal god. This caused a real problem for both the Jews, who lived throughout the empire, and the Christians. Other Romans, who still loyally believed in the emperor cult, were willing to do whatever the government asked and didn't see why others were not also willing. The Romans excused the Jews from worshipping the Roman gods because Judaism had been around for so long. But the Christians were new and were therefore regarded with suspicion. Also, the Romans had heard terrible rumors about the Christians. These rumors included one that accused them of killing their children and eating them.

Prejudice against Christians grew. Near the end of his reign, Diocletian passed laws that made the practice of Christianity dangerous:

> Royal edicts [proclamations] were published everywhere, commanding that the churches should be razed to the ground, the Scriptures destroyed by fire, those who held positions of honor degraded, and

In the nineteenth century, the Italian artist Mancinelli painted this depiction of the slaughter of Christians in the catacombs (underground cemeteries) of ancient Rome. Christianity became illegal during the reign of Diocletian.

WHAT'S YOUR SIGN?

As the difficult third century progressed, Romans began to believe that their gods had turned against them. The empire was no longer in favor. To avoid bad luck, many people looked to the night sky for help. The patterns of the stars were thought to warn people of events to come. The Romans were not alone in their belief in the stars and their meaning. Most of the ancient world searched the night sky for help in avoiding disasters.

A Roman zodiac wheel (above) *is just one example of the Romans' belief in divine messages from the skies.*

the household servants, if they persisted in the Christian profession, be deprived [put in prison].[26]

Diocletian declared Christianity an illegal religion and set out to punish its followers. The bishops and other clergy became his favorite targets.

EFFECTS OF DIOCLETIAN'S REFORMS

Some of the effects of Diocletian's reforms were good. The reforms helped to steady the empire for the twenty years of his reign. In some ways, life improved for the people. For instance, Diocletian regulated the production of coins. He ruled that coins made in different areas of the empire were to contain the same amount of precious metals (such as gold and silver). He also made sure that every coin bore a mark indicating where it was minted. That way, if it didn't contain the right amount of gold or other metal, a coin could be traced back to its source. This may have helped to restore the people's confidence in the money system and kept trade from declining. Diocletian also stopped the use of the military police that had been terrorizing private citizens. By A.D. 298, the army had pushed the Goths back across the Rhine and Danube borders and stopped the Sassanid advance in the eastern provinces.

Diocletian's changes also had some bad effects on the empire and its population. These bad effects may have been made worse by the fact that his subjects had little loyalty to him and resisted his reforms. Diocletian's changes favored the army at the public's expense. The habit of placing the welfare of his soldiers above that of the citizens got worse under his rule. This favoring of the troops changed the social structure of the empire. The military became the privileged class. The emperor's men rose to become provincial officials, military officers, and even emperors themselves. They crowded out the middle class and grabbed the prestige and power that had once belonged to the Senate.

DIOCLETIAN'S BATHS

Even though Diocletian was unpopular, the people of Rome loved the baths he built for them. These baths were the biggest and most luxurious in the ancient world. As many as three thousand bathers could use them at one time. They provided the people with libraries, steam rooms, gardens, and even heated toilets. Diocletian used the labor of five hundred slaves to construct the baths.

In the sixteenth century, the Italian artist Michelangelo adapted one section of the baths of Diocletian for the Basilica of Saint Mary of the Angels and Martyrs in Rome. This photograph shows one of the entrances into the basilica through the original Roman stonework.

Although Diocletian gave the senators back their tax-free status, he did not give them back any real power or purpose. The Senate had not passed a law since A.D. 280. The people, including the wealthy minority, were no longer represented in the government.

When Diocletian declared that citizens could not change their jobs or location, he made it impossible for those who were not in the army to rise in the economic and social structure. They were locked into the place they inherited. His taxes put such a burden on middle-class citizens that many voluntarily joined the ranks of the poor. In the end, some things may have improved, but others were much worse.

After a while, it was clear that some of Diocletian's changes weren't going to work. People ignored his price guidelines in spite of his threats of execution. Many Romans also refused his religious reforms. They simply would not treat him like a god.

Other Romans didn't want to worship many different gods. When Christians refused to worship the way Diocletian told them to, he had them thrown in prison or

KEEPING THE DISTANCE

To emphasize his status as emperor, Diocletian required those who wanted to speak to him to kneel before looking at him. Sometimes they had to talk to him while lying facedown on the floor.

beaten, and sometimes executed. Despite the harsh punishments, Christians continued to oppose him. At one point, Diocletian tried to make peace with the Christians by making them an offer: if those already in prison would make just one small sacrifice to the Roman gods, they could go free. The historian Lacantius described the offer this way:

> The first decrees were followed by others
> commanding that those in prison should be set free,
> if they would sacrifice, but that those who refused
> should be tormented with countless tortures. [27]

Romans also disliked the fact that Diocletian's laws were not evenly enforced throughout the empire. In some places, the prisons became overcrowded with Christians. The officials sent word to Diocletian that they had put so many Christians in jail, there was no longer any room for criminals. However, other officials all but ignored Diocletian and his laws.

CHAPTER FIVE

BALANCING ACT

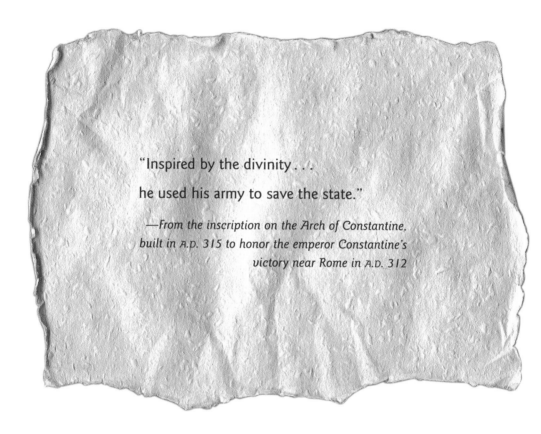

"Inspired by the divinity . . .

he used his army to save the state."

—From the inscription on the Arch of Constantine,
built in A.D. 315 to honor the emperor Constantine's
victory near Rome in A.D. 312

D iocletian's tetrarchy was supposed to transfer power
peacefully upon the death or retirement of the emperor. It
was a good plan, but it didn't work. When he left the throne
in A.D. 305, Diocletian persuaded Maximian to retire, too.
This cleared the way for the two junior emperors. One of
them was Constantius, who became western emperor in 305.
A year later, Constantius died. His troops declared

Constantine's profile appears on a coin from the beginning of his reign in A.D. 306–307.

Constantine, his son, the new emperor. Not everyone liked the choice, and the tetrarchy fell apart. This started another civil war. At least six claims were made for the throne. But in 312, Constantine emerged from the pack to face Maxentius, his main rival.

VICTORY AT MILVIAN BRIDGE

Constantine waited at the Milvian Bridge, which spans the Tiber River; the river flows along the outskirts of Rome.

A successor to the original Milvian Bridge stands in Rome after being rebuilt in the fourteenth century.

He had come with 40,000 troops to fight Maxentius for the throne. Maxentius's army was four times bigger than Constantine's. Eusebius, Constantine's biographer, described what happened shortly before the battle:

"Around noon, as the day was already moving toward its end, [Constantine] saw in the sky over the sun the sign of the [Christian] cross composed of light, with an attached writing saying ['in this, conquer']."

Constantine insisted that the light he saw was shaped like a cross. He took this vision to be a sign that the Christian God was going to help him defeat Maxentius. Constantine ordered his soldiers to paint onto their shields a

Christian symbol that would protect them in battle. When the day ended, Constantine was victorious. From this point on, he publicly praised the God of Christianity and Judaism. Milvian Bridge was the most important victory of his life. It gave him control of the western portion of the empire. The eastern portion would be his by A.D. 324.

DISPATCH OF MAXENTIUS

Constantine treated Maxentius, his rival for the western throne, without pity. After the battle, Maxentius was found floating in the Tiber River—without his head. Constantine had the head publicly displayed on top of a pole in the city of Rome.

In the early seventeenth century, the Flemish artist Peter Paul Rubens depicted the Battle of Milvian Bridge in his painting Battle of Constantine and Maxentius.

CHRISTIAN OR PAGAN?

There has been much discussion about whether Constantine became a Christian after his experience at Milvian Bridge. Although he did not allow himself to be baptized—a necessary ceremony for Christians—most current scholars think that he really did convert to Christianity. Some say that Constantine worshipped the Roman sun god. Like the God of the Jews and Christians, the Roman sun god was considered the single deity by its followers. These scholars find that the step from belief in a single pagan god to belief in the God of Christianity and Judaism wasn't a difficult one for Constantine to take.

However, there is evidence that Constantine's conversion was simply part of a balancing act he performed for both the Romans who did not follow Christianity and those who did. For example, although he built Christian churches, he minted coins during his reign that had an imprint of the Roman gods. And, although he made the practice of Christianity legal again, he also allowed the worship of Rome's traditional pagan gods.

Although the reason isn't clear, Constantine got very involved with the business of the Christian church. Some historians say his purpose was political, not religious. They believe that he wanted to keep the church happy so that as its membership and influence grew, it wouldn't work against the empire. Constantine may have hoped that the organization of the church would be a model for the empire and keep it united. For whatever reason, he gathered Christian clergy together in the city of Nicaea, in present-day Turkey, in A.D. 325, to settle certain points of disagreement.

ONE GOD OR TWO?

Early Christians debated whether Jesus was of the same substance as God. A minority of Christians didn't think so. The majority believed that Jesus *had* to be of the same substance. Otherwise, they would be worshipping more than just one God. At Nicaea, the Christians wrote a statement of Christian beliefs. This statement, called the Nicene Creed, made official their belief regarding Jesus. Jesus and God were of the same substance; therefore, there was only one God.

This eighteenth-century Russian painting shows the Council of Nicaea that took place in A.D. 325.

Some laws that Constantine issued seemed to follow the Christian teaching of kindness. New laws gave slaves some legal protection from their owners, for example. Yet Constantine passed some cruel laws, as well. He ruled, for instance, that a woman who ran away with a man who was not her husband would be set on fire as punishment. If a

EXECUTION ORDERS

In 326, Constantine ordered the execution of his wife, Fausta, and his son Crispus (from a relationship previous to his marriage). Because the executions closely followed each other, many historians think there was a link between them. There are many theories. One is that Fausta and Crispus had a love affair. Another is that they were involved in a political plot against Constantine. Whatever the reason, Fausta's execution took place in hot water. Some scholars say she was suffocated in an overheated bath. Others say she was boiled to death.

servant aided her in running away with a man, the servant could be made to swallow molten lead. Any man who raped a woman was to be burned alive—but if the woman had been raped while away from her home, she was punished, too. Constantine believed that women should stay within the protection and control of their husbands and families. And it was during his reign that the government began to torture citizens who were either unable or unwilling to pay their taxes.

MILITARY MIGHT

Constantine strengthened the army's fortifications along the Danube River where the barbarians were most likely to raid. Like Diocletian, Constantine welcomed recruits from the warring tribes. At the same time, he officially dismissed the

Praetorian Guard, which had once been powerful enough to decide who became emperor. He made Diocletian's division of the army into limitanei and comitatenses official and focused on increasing their mobility. This allowed him to move the field army closer to the empire's interior, but still keep it capable of quick and deadly strikes when needed at the borders.

In A.D. 313, Constantine agreed to rule jointly with Licinius, the eastern emperor. But the agreement didn't last long. The two were soon at war with one another for control of the empire. But as he was trying to outthink Licinius, Constantine had to watch another challenge. In

POLITICS AND RELIGION

It is possible to conclude from Constantine's actions that he was a better politician than Christian. Some historians argue that he knew the potential of the Christian church to grow in number and influence. He may have concluded that the church would either strengthen the empire or bring its downfall. The teachings of Christianity were in direct conflict with the practices of the Roman Empire. The church taught that people should be kind toward others and reject the material (or non-spiritual) world. The empire represented everything that the church said was of no real value. This included power, money, and territory. Constantine may have decided it was better to be a friend of the church than an enemy.

315, and again in 322 through 323, the Goths renewed their assaults on the borders. Constantine launched a successful defensive strike against them along 300 miles (483 km) of the frontier. He returned later to strike even more decisively, forcing the Goths to sign a treaty promising to defend the empire against other tribes. Constantine celebrated this

THE PERSIAN EMPIRES

Rome's neighbor to the east, Persia, which included today's Iran and Iraq, had been a huge empire, at least as big as the Roman Empire. Like Rome, Persia was under constant attack by nomadic tribes to the north and the east and was at war at times with the Kushans of northwestern India (present-day Afghanistan and Pakistan). The Romans and Persians had long wanted to conquer each other. In fact, for hundreds of years, they fought wars against one another. The Persians had a highly developed culture, with a written language, excellent irrigation systems, and prosperous trading. They even had a fast mail service. The quality of life was generally good. During the late Roman Empire, the Persians were ruled by the Parthians, who were not Persian. This period is sometimes called the Parthian Empire. Around A.D. 224, the Sassanid Empire began after the Parthians were defeated by the Sassanids, who were Persian. The Sassanids ruled until 640. Skilled warriors, the Parthians had caused the Romans a lot of trouble on the boundaries between the two defeat of an old enemy by issuing thousands of victory coins. But he celebrated too early. The old enemy simply moved to other areas along the borders and continued their attacks. As Constantine tried to defeat Licinius and hold back the Goths, the Sassanids attacked the eastern flank of the empire again.

empires. But the Sassanids, who had a better organized military, were a greater and more determined threat to the Romans. After Rome officially became Christian, the hostilities between the two empires increased. The Sassanids were Zoroastrians, belonging to the traditional belief system of Persia. They worshipped one god, called Ahura Mazda, and believed that life on Earth was a struggle between good and evil.

The Persian king Shahpur I fights the Roman emperor Valerian in the early third century. This cameo, a type of carved jewelry, is from the fourth century A.D.

THE NEW ROME

Constantine defeated Licinius in A.D. 324 and gained sole power over both the eastern and western divisions of the Roman Empire. He was the first to do so since Diocletian divided its territory in 286. In 330, Constantine chose the ancient Greek city of Byzantium as his official capital city. He renamed the city Constantinople (known today as Istanbul, Turkey) and laid out its new boundaries. When he was finished, the city was four times bigger than it had been. Constantine began to transform Constantinople into the "New Rome," with an ambitious public building program

The outer walls (above) of Roman Constantinople still stand in Istanbul, Turkey. Constantine's move of the capital from Rome to Constantinople irreversibly changed the Roman Empire.

that included a forum and beautiful walkways. In his capital and throughout the empire, Constantine built magnificent churches dedicated to the Christian God, not pagan deities.

Constantinople was a terrific location. The city sits on a strategically important spot near what was then the empire's Danube River boundary and within striking distance of Persian lands to the east. Not only did this location allow Constantine to watch the troubled borders of the empire, it let him see what was going on in the Mediterranean and Black seas.

Earlier emperors had used various cities in Italy and the provinces for their base of operations, including Milan, Trier, and Thessalonika. These shifts of power gradually reduced Rome's influence as the center of government. The shift to the "New Rome" reduced the influence of the "Old Rome" even further. For one thing, many wealthy and educated Romans followed the emperor to Constantinople and found the city more to their liking. And, even though Constantine was the only emperor, the move to the East emphasized how much weaker Rome and the West were— economically, politically, and militarily.

JULIAN THE APOSTATE

When Constantine died in 337, the government issued coins stamped with the phrase, "The Peace of the Emperors." These words may have given some Romans hope that the transfer of power would be smooth. It wasn't. Like other emperors, Constantine tried but failed to command the future. His three sons inherited the empire, but his nephew Julian gained sole control in 361.

Julian the Apostate restored the Roman Empire to paganism. In this marble statue from the fourth century, Julian wears the cloak of Greek philosophers and the crown of pagan cults.

Constantine's true religious beliefs may remain a mystery, but nobody doubts Julian's. He was a pagan. As emperor he tried his best to stop what his uncle had begun: the special privileges of the Christian church.

The fact that Christians wouldn't pay respect to Rome's deities or emperors became an issue among pagan Romans when the empire was on the decline. Between the reigns of Constantine and Julian, during the years 337 to 360, the Christian church rose in power. It persuaded the

SAINT CONSTANTINE

The Eastern Orthodox Church holds Constantine in great respect. He is one of its revered saints. The church has set aside two days of its calendar each year to honor him: May 21, a day he shares with his mother, who was also a Christian, and September 3. It was the Christian church that gave him his best-known name: Constantine the Great.

government to close many of the pagan temples and even to condemn the tradition of emperor-worship. The church also set out to close down another Roman institution: the Colosseum and its replicas throughout the empire.

Julian thought these Christian restrictions hurt the unity of the empire. The pagan temples and the Colosseum games had been among the important connections holding together the varied cultures of the Roman world. He reversed the laws unfavorable to the pagans. As they had for his uncle, the Christians gave Julian a new name: Julian the Apostate, which means "Julian who has Forsaken the Faith." But Julian posed only a temporary threat to Christianity. In 363, while trying to decisively defeat the Persians, he was killed in battle.

CHAPTER SIX

THE MIGRATION

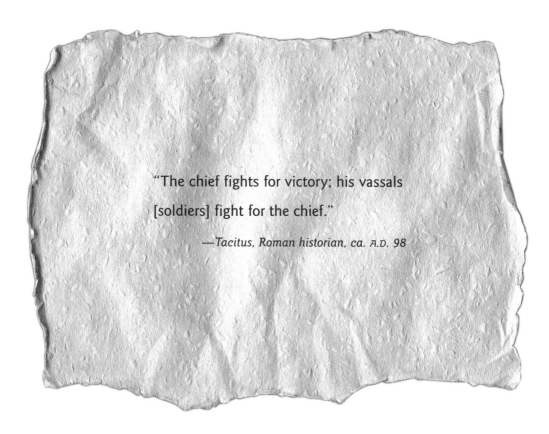

"The chief fights for victory; his vassals
[soldiers] fight for the chief."

—*Tacitus, Roman historian, ca. A.D. 98*

By the end of Emperor Julian's short reign (A.D. 361–363), Rome and its barbarian neighbors had slipped into a familiar, if not comfortable, pattern. The tribes continually raided any weak spot along the empire's borders, and the Roman soldiers hurried to push them back. In spite of the ongoing conflict, the Romans and the barbarians worked out certain mutually satisfactory arrangements. Of

ROMANS AND RECRUITS

By the fourth century A.D., Roman soldiers no longer had the respect or admiration of the citizens. The army found it difficult to find recruits. Some Christians refused to join on moral grounds. But non-Christians, too, looked for ways to avoid the military. One of these ways became common practice: men cut off their own thumbs so they would be unacceptable to the military. Since Roman landowners were required to supply the army with a certain number of recruits from their workforce, the army changed their quota. Landowners would be required to supply two men who were missing a thumb for every one who was not.

course, the Romans always needed soldiers for their army, and the barbarians were their major source of recruitment. But there was also a lot of trade across the boundaries. For example, the barbarians got necessities, such as grains, wine, and cloth, from the Romans. And the Romans happily accepted slaves in return. In some ways, the empire and its closest barbarian neighbors grew dependent on each other.

By the late third century A.D., various Germanic tribes were settled in areas near the European borders of the empire. The Franks, for example, were northwest of the empire, and the Burgundians were south of the Franks. The Alamanni were just beyond the Rhine River as it bordered northeastern Gaul.

The Goths were farther east than most other tribes, spread out over a vast area. Some of their people settled along the borders of the Roman province of Dacia. After Rome abandoned the province as ungovernable, many of the Goths moved into Dacia. Other Goths settled farther east along the coast of the Black Sea.

Until the fourth century, the Germanic tribes had never presented a unified force. They had no desire to take over and settle the lands they conquered in battle. They had made some very effective strikes, including the destruction of major cities in the empire. And, in the third century, they had launched several major attacks. Their method of warfare had always been the same: a surprise attack, a thorough razing (destruction) of the land if the tribes won the battle, and then temporary retreat. When not fighting the Romans, these tribes roamed the lands in small groups that often fought one another.

THE MIGHTY GOTHS

The Goths raided the Roman province of Dacia in A.D. 251, defeating the army led by the emperor Decius. Decius announced to his troops that the loss of a single soldier was of little importance. This was just after his son was killed in the battle. Decius was killed shortly after and his troops were badly defeated. The empire abandoned the province of Dacia as indefensible.

WHY ALL THE FIGHTING?

Like the Romans, the barbarians gloried in their battle skills. Even their games were warlike, giving them a chance to sharpen their fighting abilities. But often they were really at war, sometimes with each other. Since family was the strongest bond in their social structure, any insult to kin needed to be answered. In addition, the tribes were often desperately competing against one another for food and shelter.

THE DREADED HUNS

Scholars agree that around A.D. 375–376, the Huns began to migrate westward from Asia, moving across what is now the European continent. Nobody knows for certain why they were migrating. However, there are a number of possibilities. Like many migrants, they may have been looking for better food and shelter. An intense climate change in the north may have made growing crops and keeping livestock difficult. Some historians think that groups such as the Huns and Goths first approached the Roman Empire because they had heard of its great wealth and wanted it. Whatever the reason, the Hun migration was not a peaceful one. The Huns attacked every tribe in their way, destroying villages, towns, and small encampments with horrifying speed and violence. They were masters of the surprise attack, superb horsemen, and deadly accurate with their bows and arrows. When attacking their enemies, they first charged them on horseback, then retreated briefly

HOMELAND OF THE HUNS

The Huns arrived on the scene totally by surprise. Other tribes, as well as the Romans, were not prepared for them. No one had ever heard of the Huns. They were not Germanic. Some scholars think they may have been related to the Hsiung-Nu people who lived in western China during the early Han dynasty (206 B.C.–A.D. 8). About fifty thousand Hsiung-Nu families are known to have migrated to the steppes (dry, grassy plains) north of the Caspian Sea.

to confuse them. The final step was setting a trap and killing their opponents in an ambush. Stories of the terrible brutality of these unfamiliar people traveled ahead of them across Europe and into the Roman Empire. The Greek historian Ammianus Marcellinus described the Huns as "two-legged beasts" in the shape of [men].

The Goths, among the first tribes to encounter the Huns, saw them much as Ammianus did. They were short and stooped, but broad-chested. Their arms were long and muscular. Their eyes were wild. To the Goths, they were terrifying. By A.D. 370, the Huns had defeated the eastern Goths, as well as other tribes. Next, the Huns headed for the western Goths, who turned to the Romans for help. In 376, hordes of Goths gathered on the edge of the Danube River where it bordered the Roman province of Thrace. They were waiting to be admitted to the relative safety of the empire. Ammianus described the scene: "The barbarians [Goths], like beasts who had broken loose from their cages, poured unrestrainedly [freely] over the vast extent of the country."

THE DEAL

When the Goths came to the Roman province of Thrace in 376, the empire was ruled by Valens in the east and his

Valens, pictured in relief on a fourth-century coin, reigned as emperor of Rome for fourteen years.

nephew Gratian in the west. According to Ammianus, when the Goths crossed the Danube into Thrace, they came as a group, under the leadership of their chosen chieftains. Appealing to Valens for shelter, they offered a deal: if they could settle within the empire's borders, they would help defend the Romans to the death against the Huns.

The Romans had heard the rumors about the strange new warriors coming from the East, soundly defeating any tribes who stood in their way. The Huns were so dreaded that other barbarians fled their homes rather than face them.

Valens accepted the deal offered by the Goths and had his men ferry them across the river. He was in great need of soldiers to support his military campaigns and was counting on plenty of recruits. But it did not take long for the deal between Valens and the Goths to go sour.

The desperate Goths came in such great numbers that the Romans couldn't keep count. According to Ammianus, who was at the scene, nobody knew how many there were.

HOW MANY IS TOO MANY?

There is no reliable record of the number of barbarians seeking shelter within the empire in 376. But some estimates are as high as 200,000. The Romans had planned on a limited migration of Goths. But the Goths were followed by other tribes—including, by some accounts, even the Huns—and the numbers swelled. The Romans were unprepared for this influx of people.

He quoted the poet Virgil, saying, "[It] was like counting . . . the waves in the African Sea."

Historical accounts say that Roman officers mistreated the Goths. Ammianus reports:

> When the barbarians who had been conducted across the river were in great distress from want of provisions, [certain Roman officers brought dogs to them to eat, and] exchanged them for an equal number of slaves.

The Roman military officers and local Thracian officials were said to have been the most abusive. Roman officers attempted to select only certain Goths for passage across the Danube. The sick, the disabled, and the defenseless were left without help outside the empire's borders to face the Huns on their own. Things weren't much better for the Goths who were taken into the empire. Famine hit the area in Thrace where they were encamped. Some families became so desperate that they sold children into slavery in return for food. While guests of the Romans, several of the Goths' leaders were killed. In addition, the empire was unable to provide the provisions and land promised by the emperor. Many of the Goths died while under the protection of the empire. The stage was set for Roman disaster at Adrianopolis.

Under Fritigern, a greatly admired chieftain, the Goths unified and rebelled. They began by rioting locally and defeating the soldiers sent by Valens, who was busy with other military campaigns. This began a period known as the Gothic Wars (A.D. 376–378).

THE BATTLE OF ADRIANOPOLIS

After winning the skirmishes with the first wave of Roman soldiers sent by Valens, the Goths stormed across Thrace, terrifying the local people. They took whatever they could by force and destroyed the rest before they retreated to regroup. The warriors' numbers were increased along the way by runaway slaves, as well as Roman citizens and others who had been ruined by the empire's policies. As the Romans pursued the Goths, destruction and suffering were everywhere. Ammianus described the chaos:

> Women panic-stricken, beaten with cracking [clubs]; some even in pregnancy. . . . Virgins and chaste matrons were dragged along with faces [twisted] by bitter weeping. . . .

Ammianus went on to explain how the Goths, in their fury, tortured and killed anyone they caught. He recalled the fate of a once-prosperous Thracian:

> [The man] was dragged along like a wild beast, [knowing he was] either to be torn from limb to limb . . . or else to be exposed to scourging [whipping] and torture.

When Fritigern sent a message to other barbarians for help, various tribes sped to his aid. According to some historians, these tribes included Huns. Together, this quickly formed army became the most determined force the Romans would ever meet. As Ammianus put it, the Romans had never truly seen what rage and despair could do.

The result was the Battle of Adrianopolis, named after a nearby Thracian city (now Edime, Turkey). In 378, Valens foolishly led his men against the Goths without waiting for reinforcements. He had grown impatient waiting for Gratian and his army and wondered whether the delay was deliberate. He suspected the western emperor of wanting to reunite the two halves of the empire under his own rule.

DELAY OR BETRAYAL?

Historians don't know for certain whether Gratian deliberately stalled in coming to Valens's defense. To gain more power, Gratian may have wanted Valens to lose the fight against the Goths. But there is evidence that Gratian and his reinforcements were delayed trying to stop other barbarian warriors, such as the Alamanni, from going to the Goths' defense. And he sent word to Valens to wait for his help. The night before the battle, Fritigern sent Valens a message asking for a peaceful settlement. Fritigern's offer to negotiate may have been sincere. It is also possible that he was buying time until the cavalry crucial to the Goths' victory arrived. Valens refused. The Goths tried diplomacy again just before the battle began. But Valens returned word that he could not take seriously any promises made by the low-ranking messengers Fritigern had sent.

Valens did not take the advice of his military officers and decided to strike with the men he had.

The battle between the Goths and Romans began in earnest in August 378. It quickly became a hand-to-hand struggle, the men so crowded against one another that at times they could not draw their weapons. As Ammianus described the scene, "the two lines of battle dashed against each other, like the rams of warships, and thrusting with all their might, were tossed to and fro like the waves of the sea . . . . [S]uch clouds of dust arose that it was barely possible to see the sky which resounded with horrible cries."

After an initial retreat, the Romans fought well. But they had both physical and psychological disadvantages. Before the battle, they had trudged for a day, carrying heavy armor and provisions in extreme heat.

Ammianus described the frightening zeal of the tribal warriors: ". . . the barbarian towering in his fierceness, hissing or shouting, falls with his legs pierced through, or his right hand cut off, sword and all, or his side transfixed

A THEORY ON THE HEAVY ROMAN LOSSES

At Adrianopolis, it is possible that some Roman soldiers, who lacked the discipline of the earlier legionaries, refused to carry the armor that might have protected them in battle and reduced the army's casualties. In addition, the Romans had underestimated the numbers and determination of the enemy.

[pierced], and still, in the last gasp of life, casting round him defiant glances."

Ammianus went on to give the details of the battlefield after the fighting ended:

> The ground, covered with streams of blood, made [the Roman soldiers'] feet slip . . . and with such vehemence [force] did they resist their enemies who pressed on them, that some were even killed by their own weapons. At last one black pool of blood disfigured everything, and wherever the eye turned, it could see nothing but piled up heaps of dead, and lifeless corpses trampled without mercy. . . .

The Battle of Adrianopolis left the Roman forces in ruins. Valens had been killed, along with three-quarters of the eastern army's men. Fending for themselves, the Roman survivors scattered in every direction. Their enemies, on the other hand, turned their sights on the nearby city of Adrianopolis. Ammianus wrote that, the morning after the battle, "the conquerors, like wild beasts rendered still more savage by the blood they had tasted . . . marched in a dense column toward Adrianopolis." A bloody attack on the city followed.

Most modern historians believe that the Huns were among the tribes who fought alongside the Goths at Adrianopolis. Some say the Huns led the barbarians in their decisive defeat of the Romans. Regardless of which tribes took part, this brutal battle set into motion events that would bring down the empire.

CHAPTER SEVEN

THE DEFEAT OF THE WESTERN ROMAN EMPIRE

"In this way, through the turbulent zeal of violent people, the ruin of the Roman [E]mpire was brought on."

—*Greek historian Ammianus Marcellinus, A.D. 376*

In 379 the Romans appointed Theodosius I to replace Valens. A native of Spain, Theodosius was a capable military man, and he became sole emperor of both the eastern and western empires in 394. From the outset, Theodosius recognized that if the Goths banded together in a united front, he would never defeat them. So he secretly approached individual chieftains, bringing flattery and gifts

Theodosius I (above on throne) *saw the Goths as a serious threat to the empire. He worked to make peace with them. This illustration is from a ninth-century manuscript.*

and asking them to break their unity with the other tribes. He urged them each to seek individual power, rather than sharing power with others. The tactic seemed to work. According to Eunapius, a fifth-century historian and eyewitness, the Gothic chieftains "were all puffed by the imperial honors and saw all power in their own hands."

Theodosius then set about solving what he saw as the empire's biggest problem: the army's loss of confidence after Adrianopolis. Again, he used a good military tactic. By entering the empire's forces into a series of short and easily won confrontations with weaker individual tribes, he gradually strengthened the morale of his troops.

Finally, Theodosius signed a treaty with the Goths, giving them a status known as *federatti* (allies). This agreement made him the first emperor to give the barbarians the right to set up an independent state within the empire's borders. The Goths could now officially govern themselves inside the empire and form their own armies, under the

THEODOSIUS THE GREAT

On the home front, Theodosius focused his energies on strengthening the church. A devout Christian, he did what Constantine would not. He outlawed worship of all Roman gods and declared the eastern empire a Christian state. This began a period of harsh treatment toward non-Christians, which would continue until the end of the empire. With his help, the Christian bishops were on their way to becoming the most powerful force in the eastern empire. The church rewarded the emperor with a new title: Theodosius the Great.

command of their own officers. In short, they got most of what they had requested before the battle at Adrianopolis. In return, the Goths and their armies were supposed to remain Roman federatti.

Theodosius probably believed he was right to sign the treaty. He knew he wouldn't be able to replace the soldiers lost at Adrianopolis with Romans. The treaty was meant to make up for the loss of draftees and recruits and to ensure a strong front at the empire's borders.

UNEVEN SHARES

In 395 Theodosius died, and control of the western empire passed to his eleven-year-old son Honorius. The eastern empire came under the rule of Honorius's older brother,

Arcadius. From this point on, the Roman Empire no longer had even the appearance of unity between its two halves. East and West had separate governments, laws, armies, and languages, as Greek had become the preferred language in the East. Bitter disagreements within the Christian church further divided the Romans.

The split was not an even one. The western empire had fewer people and resources. Its borders along the Rhine and Danube rivers were much more difficult to defend than those of the eastern empire, requiring many more soldiers. It did not have the vigorous trade of the eastern empire, and its people were dependent upon the provinces for food.

The eastern empire, by contrast, had Egypt and other extremely prosperous trading centers within its borders. Much of its trade took place along the Silk Road, far from the troubled routes of the west, and its agricultural lands were very productive. The lives of Romans in Constinople and other areas of the east were largely untouched by the economic and civil problems in the west.

This marble bust of the emperor Arcadius is from the fourth century B.C.

The western empire also had political troubles. Officially, the western empire was ruled by Honorius. But from 395, when his reign began, until 408, Honorius's guardian, Stilicho, made the decisions. Although he had been appointed guardian by Theodosius, Stilicho was half Vandal and half Roman. To Romans, this made him a barbarian. As a result, rivals began plotting against him as soon as Theodosius died, and possibly even before.

This Roman ivory carving from the early fifth century shows the emperor Honorius holding a sign that says in Latin "In the name of Christ you will always win."

Theodosius was not the only one who saw the danger of the barbarians uniting under a single ruler. The battle at Adrianopolis had shown the Goths, too, just how lethal their tribes could be when joined together to fight a common enemy. The huge victory they had won over the Romans at Adrianopolis marked the beginning of the end of the western empire. The army would never recover, and the western empire's lands slowly fell into barbarian hands.

THE SACKING OF ROME AND OTHER LOSSES

The change in the relationship between the tribes and the empire was obvious from the treaty signed by Theodosius. Critics of the treaty thought it was foolish for the Romans to believe that the barbarians owed any loyalty to the empire. Allowing the tribes to have their own leaders would almost guarantee their betrayal of Rome. Many historians think that the Romans badly underestimated their status in the barbarian world following Adrianopolis.

The critics were right. When Theodosius died in 395, the Goths considered themselves free of the treaty and joined ranks like they had at Adrianopolis. They chose Alaric, the leader of the barbarian auxiliary troops under Theodosius, as their king. Alaric ignored the treaty entirely and in 395 led his tribes to invade Greece and the surrounding Roman provinces. The Goths destroyed Corinth, Argos, and Sparta. But for a huge bribe, they agreed not to destroy the city of Athens.

In 401, Alaric attacked the Italian peninsula. Stilicho managed, without help from the eastern empire, to fend him off. Meanwhile, Honorius fled to safety in the heavily fortified Italian city of Ravenna, and in 402 made it the western empire's capital. In order to keep Rome safe, Stilicho had to take most of his soldiers from the Rhine, leaving the European border without adequate defense. This was the cue for other barbarians to make their move. Around 406, the Vandals, now joined with the Alans, invaded Gaul. In doing so, these barbarian tribes destroyed much of the agriculture on which the western empire depended. From Gaul, they crossed the Pyrenees Mountains (along the border between present-day France and Spain) into Iberia (modern-day Spain).

When Alaric threatened Rome again in 407, Stilicho urged Honorius to negotiate with the Gothic king and pay the ransom being demanded. In return, Alaric had agreed to withdraw his army.

THE ALANS

The Alans (or Alani) were a nomadic group that was Persian, not Germanic. After being pushed westward by the Huns during the migration of 370, they split into groups. One of these groups joined with the Vandals, and together they made raids on the Roman Empire. Ammianus described the Alans relatively positively. They were, he said, tall and blond, but had fierce eyes.

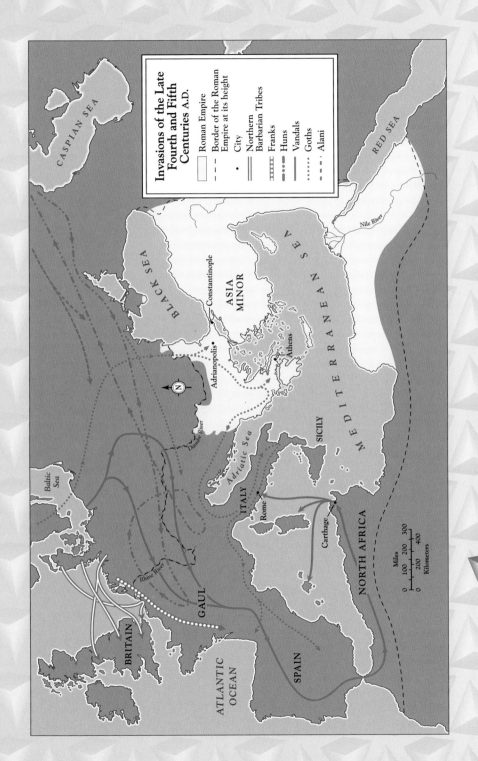

Invasions of the Late
Fourth and Fifth
Centuries A.D.

Roman Empire

Border of the Roman
Empire at its height

• City

Northern
Barbarian Tribes

Franks

Huns

Vandals

Goths

Alani

N

CASPIAN SEA

BLACK SEA

Constantinople

ASIA
MINOR

Adrianopolis

Athens

RED SEA

Nile River

MEDITERRANEAN SEA

Adriatic Sea

Danube River

Baltic
Sea

Rhine River

ITALY

Rome

SICILY

Carthage

NORTH AFRICA

Miles
0   100 200 300
0   200 400
Kilometers

BRITAIN

ATLANTIC
OCEAN

GAUL

SPAIN

But in response to the barbarian invasions, anti-barbarian groups were growing more vocal in Rome. In 408, Honorius, possibly urged on by Stilicho's many critics, ordered Stilicho executed. After all, he was half barbarian and *could* have cooperated secretly with fellow barbarian Alaric. Or perhaps Stilicho had been promised a percentage of the bribe. Nobody knows exactly why Honorius ordered Stilicho's execution. Some historians think that he was responding to a rumor that Stilicho planned to place his own son on the throne. Whatever Honorius's reason, Stilicho was beheaded. His death left the western empire without an effective leader against the barbarian tribes.

The possibility that there had been some type of a conspiracy between Alaric and Stilicho prompted the Romans to turn violent against the barbarians, especially those in northern Italy. The execution also enraged the Goths, causing mutinies among those who still served the Roman army. In addition, as many as thirty thousand new barbarian warriors joined Alaric, hoping to avenge Stilicho's death.

Some historical accounts place Alaric and his men, who included a group of Huns, outside Rome in the summer of 409. Rather than trying to force his men over the walls into the city, Alaric tried a different strategy. He would starve the Romans into submission. His men surrounded the walls and no one was allowed to enter or leave the city. Then Alaric set up a blockade, cutting off Rome from Portus, the delivery point for Egyptian grain and olive oil shipments. As the citizens of Rome struggled to survive, sickness spread through the city, increasing their suffering. Although urged by the Senate to compromise and offer Alaric an alliance, Honorius refused. Alaric's patience ran out in August 410, and he struck the starving city. The attack on Rome lasted from three to seven days, according to different accounts.

Eighteenth century historian Edward Gibbon described the state of the people before Alaric attacked:

> [They] experienced the distress of scarcity and at length the horrid calamities of famine. The daily allowance of three pounds of bread was reduced to one-half, to one-third, to nothing; and the price of corn . . . [rose] in a rapid and extravagant proportion.

Alaric and the Goths enter Rome in 410 A.D. They lay siege to Rome for over a year before striking the city.

The poorer citizens, who were unable to purchase
the necessaries of life, [pleaded for] the [unreliable]
charity of the rich. . . . A dark suspicion was
entertained that some desperate wretches had fed on
the bodies of their fellow-creatures.

Rome waited in vain for help from Constantinople, the
capital of the eastern empire. Arcadius had promised
repeatedly to send troops to reinforce the western army. But
some modern scholars think Arcadius never intended to
save the Romans. Instead, they think that he was financing
Alaric and his siege on Rome. Conspiracy or not, according
to Gibbon, the Romans starved:

Many thousands of the inhabitants of Rome expired
in their houses or in the streets for want of
sustenance . . . and the stench that arose from so
many putrid [rotten] and unburied carcasses infected
the air, and the miseries of the famine
were . . . aggravated by . . . disease.

Augustine, a Christian bishop, wrote the church's
account of the attack:

All the devastation, the butchery, the
plundering . . . were in accordance with the general
practice of warfare. But there was something
which . . . changed the whole aspect of the scene; the
savagery of the barbarians took on such an aspect
that the largest churches were . . . set aside to be

THE FRANKS

Despite the activity of the Goths, it was the Franks who had the biggest impact on modern Europe. Like the western Goths, they accepted federatti status with the Romans. But by the end of the fifth century, they had taken control of almost all of Gaul. Their language, based on Latin, evolved into modern-day French.

filled with people to be spared. . . . This is to be attributed to the name of Christ and the influence of Christianity.

Modern scholars think the Goths were actually quite restrained during the attack. Many Gothic warriors had become Christians themselves and hesitated to show disrespect for the church property or those sheltered inside the churches.

The warriors left with a great deal of plunder, but did not destroy the ancient heart of the old empire. Not since the Celts, eight centuries earlier, had an enemy force breached the walls of the city of Rome.

THE WESTERN EMPIRE FALLS

The ancient world was shattered by the sacking of Rome, even though the great city had already lost its status as the center of civilization. People were outraged at the idea of barbarians torching the ground sacred to both Christians and pagans. But there was little they could do. The Goths abandoned the city of Rome and headed south in search of food. Their goal was northern Africa, which was rich in agricultural products of all kinds. But when they put to sea, their boats sank in a storm. Then their beloved leader, Alaric, died suddenly. Mourning their fallen king, the troops returned to Italian soil and abandoned their Christian practices in order to give him a pagan burial. They left him buried in a riverbed with golden treasures to help him to the afterlife.

GALLA PLACIDIA, UNOFFICIAL EMPRESS OF ROME

Beginning in the mid-420s, the western empire was not ruled by an emperor. It was ruled by an empress, although she did not formally hold that title. Aelia Galla Placidia was the daughter of Theodosius I and half sister to the emperors Honorius and Arcadius. She was captured by the Goths sometime prior to their sacking of Rome in 410 and was married to Athaulf, successor to Alaric. Their son, Theodosius, might have bound the Goths and Romans in a new, united empire had he not died in infancy. But Placidia made decisions for the Western Roman Empire for almost ten years (425–433), until her son Valentinian III was deemed old enough to rule. During this time, she appointed

At this time, according to Edward Gibbon, the Vandals and other tribes had already crossed the Pyrenees Mountains into Iberia unchallenged. Roman troops had been called home to defend the empire's European frontier, leaving the Iberian Peninsula (present-day Spain and Portugal) defended only by local militias. They were no match for the Vandals. The Romans lost Iberia. And even without Alaric, the Goths were increasing in strength and power. In 418, they set up their own kingdom in Gaul's Aquitaine province. Bit by bit, the

many of the military leaders and church officials throughout the empire. A devout Christian, she also built or restored a number of churches.

This fifth-century A.D. medallion shows Galla Placidia (right) and two of her children.

barbarian tribes were taking apart the western empire and dividing it among themselves.

The Huns had also been busy grabbing territory under their king, Attila. By 434 this powerful leader reigned over a vast kingdom, reaching from central Europe to the Black Sea, and from the non-Roman side of the Danube River to the Baltic Sea. Many of the Goths were now under his rule.

Attila made a treaty with the Romans in 434 that should have kept the Huns on their side of the Danube permanently. But he broke the treaty around 440, possibly because the Roman frontier stood almost undefended while the Roman

ATTILA AT HOME

Although said to be a vicious warrior, Attila's personal life seems to have been quite reserved and orderly. According to the eastern Roman historian Priscus, Attila lived simply, without adornment, and his manner was quiet. Sent by Rome to Attila as a diplomat, Priscus described a Hun banquet:

A luxurious meal, served on silver plate, had been made ready for us and the barbarian guests, but Attila ate nothing but meat on a wooden trencher [platter]. In everything else, too, he showed himself [to be mild of manner and modest]; his cup was of wood, while the guests' were of gold and silver. His dress, too, was quite simple, [aiming] only to be clean.

army was trying (unsuccessfully) to save Carthage, in North Africa, from the Vandals. Seeing that there was little to stand in their way, Attila and his men charged from west to east across the provinces, destroying everything in their path. Outside the walls of Constantinople, they defeated the Roman army and were paid a huge amount of gold to go away. Under the ferocious Attila, the Huns became known as Europe's monsters.

This nineteenth-century illustration by French artist Alphonse de Neuville shows Attila (center with shield) and the Huns in battle. De Neuville made the Huns look like the monsters they were reported to be.

Overall, the fifth century was a time of confused alliances. Regional armies consisted of various peoples, including Romans, Goths, Huns, and others. In 451, Attila was stopped at Châlons, Gaul, by an alliance of Roman and Gothic armies. The battle that followed involved more than 1 million men and caused an estimated 300,000 casualties. In the end, it was the Romans' last great victory—but Attila almost immediately reinvaded northern Italy.

Although the Huns left nothing standing wherever they went, they did not take Rome. At the Po River, north of Rome, Attila was met by officials of the empire and the church—a clear sign of both the power and the political involvement of the Christians. Historians don't know how, but the group convinced Attila to retreat and leave Italy. Then, when Attila died suddenly in 453, his kingdom fell apart.

By this time, however, there was little left of the Roman Empire. The Romans even withdrew from Great Britain in 442, following the arrival of still more barbarian tribes—the Angles, the Saxons, and the Jutes. The Western Roman Empire controlled only the Italian peninsula and a few small areas on the European boundaries, and even these had no real security.

There was also little left of the distinction between "Roman" and "barbarian." Aetius, a Roman who spent much of his youth among the Huns, challenged the empress Placidia for power. He took charge around 433 to 435, but was soon threatened by Gaiseric (also called Genseric), one of the great Vandal kings. The empire passed back and forth between a series of barbarians and Roman leaders with barbarian ties until it fell to Orestes, a Roman who had been secretary to Attila the Hun. Orestes placed his son, Romulus Augustulus, on the throne of the western empire in Ravenna. But in 476, Romulus Augustulus was deposed (removed) by Odoacer, a Gothic king who had once been a general in the Roman army.

Romulus Augustulus is considered the last ruler of the Western Roman Empire. The Eastern Roman Empire still prospered. But for all its previous glory and power, the Roman Empire had fallen.

W CHAPTER EIGHT
WHEN THE CENTER DOES NOT HOLD

Turning and turning in the widening gyre [spiral]

The falcon cannot hear the falconer;

Things fall apart; the center cannot hold;

Mere anarchy [chaos] is loosed upon the world. . . .

—W. B. Yeats, from the poem "The Second Coming," 1919

Many modern historians believe that the Roman Empire slid rather than fell. Nevertheless, most agree that A.D. 476 was a pivotal moment in history. Nothing could take the place of the Roman Empire as a unifying force in Europe. Average Romans of the time probably weren't aware of it, but they were witnessing the end of the classical world.

THE CLASSICAL WORLD

The term "classical world" refers to the ideals of the ancient Greeks and Romans who dominated the Mediterranean area from around 500 B.C. to A.D. 476. At its peak, the classical world valued reason, order, balance, and simplicity. These characteristics affected every aspect of life, including philosophy, religion, art, literature, politics, architecture, public policy, foreign policy—even clothing.

Although it did not stop, Western Civilization greatly slowed down after 476. The ability to unite and govern diverse people over great distances was gone. Long before the abrupt departure of Romulus Augustulus, the empire had failed to protect its people under both its system of laws and its military. The army had shown that it could not even protect the city of Rome. As it struggled to support an ineffective, divided army, the empire's economy sank, taking its transportation network down with it. This stopped the free exchange of goods, services, knowledge—and new ideas. These factors, in turn, made cultural and religious tolerance less likely and restricted educational and artistic development. Other connections that made people feel they were part of the larger empire, such as a common language, traditional ceremonies and games, and a collective pride in their civilization, were also lost.

After 476, life didn't change suddenly for the average Roman. Although now under barbarian rule, the rich

In this early fourth-century mosaic, a Roman lady (center) goes to the baths accompanied by her servants. After the Roman empire fell, the gap between rich and poor increased.

continued their long-held practice of retreating to huge country estates. There they prospered through the labor of the poor and the enslaved. Around their self-sufficient estates they built huge walls, which they took care to fortify heavily. The gap between the classes grew steadily. The poor continued to suffer, although some would be given shelter by the church. Romans still struggled to pay their taxes, and, on average, they still died before the age of thirty.

Gibbon wrote that, at their peak, Romans had surely experienced the happiest and most prosperous period in the history of the world. But, as later historians note, even during the Pax Romana there were millions of people under the empire's rule who could not possibly have described themselves as either happy or prosperous, especially the realm's many slaves. And the lives of the poor were almost as difficult. Those in the countryside, who barely produced enough to survive, were taxed at the same rate as wealthy owners of productive land. By the fourth century, all farmers were paying three times the taxes they had twenty years earlier. Gangs of desperate men who had been broken by harsh state policies roamed the countryside. Often in league with barbarian raiders, they robbed citizens, who were left undefended. Although population statistics from ancient Rome are not reliable, some historians think that the number of people living in the western empire declined at least 20 percent between A.D. 250 and 400.

Still, the memory, or myth, of Rome remained, and others tried but failed to recapture the empire's glory. This included certain officials of the Christian church. After 476, Christianity was still the dominant religion in the western empire, having added many barbarian converts. It did not have the unifying power of the empire, but through its common belief system, it did unify its many followers across geographic, cultural, and economic lines. The church's wealth, as well as its influence in state issues, increased dramatically during the later years of the empire. At times the church negotiated for later emperors, especially with the barbarians who had turned to Christianity. The church also governed certain cities, collected taxes, and had its own courts of law. It took over some social services, such as feeding the poor.

But, according to some historians, the church seemed more interested in the material world than in compassion and goodness. Some clerics (members of the clergy), horrified at the church's direction, dedicated themselves to the poor and sick. Some retreated to monasteries where they quietly kept the knowledge and languages of the classical world alive. Yet others, especially high officials, openly competed and paid for more power in the church and government.

In 493, Odoacer was killed by his fellow Goth, Theodoric. Theodoric, along with his successor Justinian, recovered much of the Roman Empire's land in the west, as well as in northern Africa. But they were never able to glue back together the pieces of the empire. For the most part,

The Emperor Justinian (center, with bowl) stands with his retinue in this sixth-century mosaic from San Vitale Cathedral in Ravenna, Italy.

cultures remained separate, and the former empire became a collection of independent states.

Meanwhile, the cost of restoring and defending the empire's territory ruined the eastern empire's economy. After Justinian died in 565, invaders stormed the Roman frontier from every direction. The first invaders were mostly barbarian tribes and Persians, but in 634, a new threat arrived in the form of Arab Muslims. The eastern realm, by this time called the Byzantine Empire, was reduced to a few areas scattered within its former domain.

The Goths who settled on what had been Rome's European lands established important individual states, but

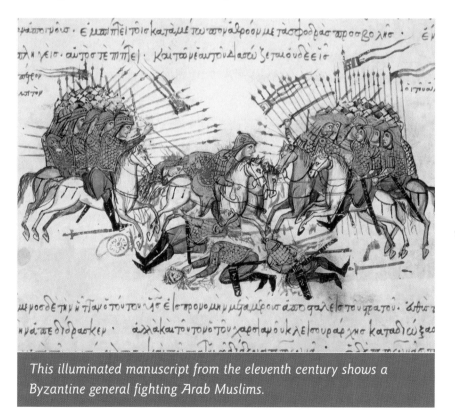

This illuminated manuscript from the eleventh century shows a Byzantine general fighting Arab Muslims.

THE MIDDLE AGES AND BEYOND

The period after 476 was once known as the Dark Ages (around A.D. 500 to around A.D. 1000), since earlier historians believed that civilization ceased to develop after the Roman Empire fell. But the period is now usually called the Early Middle Ages (with the Middle Ages extending from around 1000 to about 1500), because scholars know that not all the light of civilization went out in 476.

In the 1300s, Western Civilization's Renaissance (rebirth) began, overlapping with the Middle Ages. A period of the great flowering of art, language, and science, the Renaissance lasted into the 1600s. It happened partly because of the Romans. As

they evolved for the most part without any real union among them. The Vandals, after spectacular military defeats of the Romans in northern Africa and other regions of the empire, scattered among the general population. After the Huns' explosive entry into the Roman world, they seemed to burn out quietly, leaving the other tribes unchallenged.

But the Franks, one of the Germanic tribes, built a new kingdom, the Carolingian Empire. They regarded it as the new Roman Empire. Under Charlemagne, their king from 771 to 814, they restored principles of government, law, education, and civic loyalty. At its largest, this empire manuscripts written by Greeks and Romans were discovered and restored by monks, classical poetic and prose forms, along with classical ideas, were learned by new generations. The remains of Roman art and architecture strongly influenced Europe and, eventually, the Americas. Until only a few generations ago, people who desired to be truly educated needed to know Latin. A look through Spanish, Italian, French, and even English dictionaries shows how greatly Latin influenced the development of many modern languages. In the twenty-first century, many countries use Roman law as the basis for their own legal systems. In countries such as the United States, Roman architecture is everywhere. From small towns to the nation's capital, buildings designed on Roman models are seen supported by Roman columns.

included much of the former western Roman realm, including the modern states of France, Belgium, Luxembourg, the Netherlands, and part of Germany. But only Charlemagne could hold the Carolingian Empire together. It broke into independent states shortly after his death in 814. And in 1453, the Byzantine Empire fell to the Ottoman Turks. Other empires rose and fell, but none had as long a history or as lasting an influence as the Roman Empire.

LESSONS FROM THE EMPIRE

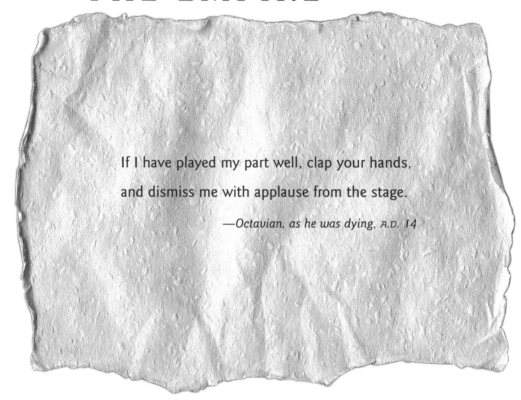

If I have played my part well, clap your hands,

and dismiss me with applause from the stage.

—*Octavian, as he was dying,* A.D. *14*

When the first Roman emperor, Octavian, counted the terrible losses at Teutoburg in A.D. 9, he was deeply shaken. For a military man, his response to the bloody ambush was unexpected. Instead of aggressive action, he pulled back his troops. It may be that Octavian knew what most of the future emperors of Rome did not: had he pushed the invaders off the land, soon they would have returned by sea.

He may have understood that his best response was to protect what was most important: the unity, confidence, and loyalty of his people. More than two thousand years ago, before the fall of what many consider the greatest empire in history, Octavian may have discovered a basic truth: even the greatest of empires will eventually fall if it loses the trust and support of its people.

PRIMARY SOURCE RESEARCH

To learn about historical events, people study many sources, such as books, websites, newspaper articles, photographs, and paintings. These sources can be separated into two general categories—primary sources and secondary sources.

A primary source is the record of an eyewitness. Primary sources provide firsthand accounts about a person or event. Examples include diaries, letters, autobiographies, speeches, newspapers, and oral history interviews. Libraries, archives, historical societies, and museums often have primary sources available on-site or on the Internet.

A secondary source is published information that was researched, collected, and written or otherwise created by someone who was not an eyewitness. These authors or artists use primary sources and other secondary sources in their research, but they interpret and arrange the source material in their own works. Secondary sources include history books, novels, biographies, movies, documentaries, and magazines. Libraries and museums are filled with secondary sources.

After finding primary and secondary sources, authors and historians must evaluate them. They may ask questions such as: Who created this document? What is this person's point of view? What biases might this person have? How trustworthy is this document? Just because a person was an eyewitness to an event does not mean that person recorded the whole truth about that event. For example, a soldier describing a battle might depict only the heroic actions of his unit and only the brutal behavior of the enemy. An account from a soldier on the opposing side might portray the same battle very differently. When sources disagree, researchers must decide through additional study which explanation makes the most sense. For this reason, historians consult a variety of primary and secondary sources. Then they can draw their own conclusions.

The Pivotal Moments in History series takes readers on a journey to important junctures in history that shaped our modern world. Authors researched each event using both primary and secondary sources, an approach that enhances readers' awareness of the complexities of the materials and helps bring to life the stories from which we draw our understanding of our shared history.

VOICES OF ANCIENT ROME

Have you ever wondered how we know what an ancient society was like? Some societies, such as that of the ancient Romans, left written records and items that citizens created or used during their everyday lives that help us understand their culture. The primary sources used in researching this book included letters, poems, battle descriptions, speeches, histories, memoirs, and other writings, many translated from Latin or some other ancient language or voice.

Educated people throughout the Roman Empire, including government workers, religious officials, scholars, geographers, and poets, left behind eyewitness accounts of the world they lived in. They recorded information about battles, religion, boundary changes, and even surgical techniques. (Roman doctors were quite advanced in treating battle wounds and left instructions for other surgeons.) The writings of people like Ammianus Marcellinus, Priscus, and Procopius provide firsthand accounts of important events in ancient Roman history. Even Roman emperors, such as Marcus Aurelius, Constantine the Great, and Julian II, wrote books, poems, satires, and official documents that tell of their accomplishments, ideas, and concerns. They also kept written government records that provide us with firsthand information. The census, for example, tells us how many citizens lived under the rule of a certain emperor. Other sources, such as grain-allotment and military records, provide what little information we have about the poor people of the empire.

Primary sources also include physical artifacts. Roman coins depict battles won, emperors' profiles, important places, and scenes or characters from Roman myths. Weapons and armor provide an idea of how Roman warfare was conducted. Household objects tell about daily life. Roads and bridges show where the Romans went and how they traveled. They also show us their great engineering skills. Works of art, such as mosaics, indicate what the Romans valued. Buildings and memorials depict their heroes and their many gods.

Important secondary sources on ancient Rome include the work of scholars of the classical era, but not necessarily eyewitnesses. For example, the Greek historian Dio Cassius wrote a gigantic study—eighty volumes long—of the

Romans. His study starts with the founding of Rome in 753 B.C. and continues to his own period (A.D. 150 to 235). Suetonius, a famous ancient historian and Roman official, wrote biographies of the first eleven emperors.

Valuable secondary sources also come from more recent writers. These studies generally offer theories about why the empire fell or make the case that the empire didn't really fall at all. How could it have fallen if its culture is part of twenty-first century culture? One of the most famous of these secondary sources is *The Decline and Fall of the Roman Empire*, written by Edward Gibbon and published between the years 1776 and 1788. Many historians still believe that this eight-volume study is the greatest work ever written about the fall of the Roman Empire. In it, Gibbon lists a number of possible causes for the fall. Among these is the cause most commonly cited: the continual assaults along the Roman borders by outsiders wanting to get in. More current studies have also been done. One, by Peter Heather, concludes that the empire fell because of the difficulty of defending its borders. But he states that the most direct cause of its fall was not the Germanic tribes, but the Persians (or Sassanids), who were an extremely determined foe.

UNDERSTANDING THE VOICES

All sources, even primary ones, need to be looked at carefully for their limitations. For example, Roman written works are almost always by and about people who were educated and wealthy. The points of view of women, the poor, and non-Romans—such as the warring tribes that played a huge role in bringing down the empire—are rarely represented. Sometimes, primary documents, such as census lists, have an unclear context. That is, the modern scholar can see population figures from a specified time but does not know what segment of the population is being counted. For instance, some census counts provide numbers on only free male property owners. That means a lot of people, such as women, children, and slaves were not counted at all.

Artifacts can easily mislead us. An emperor's profile on a coin, for instance, has almost certainly been corrected to remove any flaws. Additionally, much of the work of ancient authors comes to us as copies made on parchment during the Middle Ages, the period from about A.D. 500 to around 1500. The scribes (copiers) were often Christian monks. They tended to copy only those writings that supported their own religious beliefs. As a result, many works from the Roman Empire weren't copied. Those that were copied may have a lot of mistakes because a scribe wasn't Roman or Greek and was translating these languages.

Obtaining accurate knowledge of an ancient civilization is tricky. It becomes more difficult with an event as complex as the fall of the Roman Empire. But with a little patience and a lot of care, we can understand a great deal.

PRIMARY SOURCE: THE ARCH

FINDING YOUR OWN VOICE

Sometimes students of history can see a source in person and come to their own conclusions about what it tells them. One source that can still be seen and puzzled over is the Arch of Constantine. This huge memorial in Rome provides a confusion of messages.

After Constantine won the battle at the Milvian Bridge in A.D. 312, he is said to have promised his loyalty to Christianity. Some scholars think that this promise helped cause the empire's fall. After all, Christian teachings opposed everything the empire stood for. In spite of the close relations between church officials and the state, the church was teaching its followers to reject worldly things; in other words, things that were Roman.

Romans who still practiced the traditional state religion eventually became enemies of the Christian church. The two sides became locked in a struggle of ideas, wealth, and power. This struggle greatly reduced Roman unity. The conflict of the two sides is carved into Roman history in one of the empire's most famous structures, the arch that the Senate built in Rome to celebrate Constantine's military victory at the Milvian Bridge.

The arch was designed by an unknown architect around 316. It is partly made of pieces from other monuments of the Pax Romana. This, together with engravings of traditional Roman gods, made the arch acceptable to Romans who believed in the empire's official religion. But carved into the wall is a statement that Constantine was divinely inspired in his victory. This suggested to others that the arch was built to praise the Christian God. Scholars and historians are still debating which beliefs the arch represents.

Also in dispute is whether the arch was a sign of the empire's decline and fall. Some experts believe that the sections of the arch made in the fourth century are not as good as those made earlier. In fact, these scholars think the older sections were used because the Romans no longer had

The friezes above the individual arches on the Arch of Constantine (above) depict different scenes from the battle at the Milvian Bridge.

the skills to sculpt them. Others say the arch is a blend of Constantine's era and the earlier empire, both of which were glorious in their own way.

Scholars and students can consider these questions for themselves, either by studying the many pictures of the arch available on the Internet or in historical books, or by visiting it. The empire is gone, but the mysterious Arch of Constantine is still standing in Rome between the Colosseum and the Palatine Hill.

TIMELINE

Roman Republic

500s b.c. Romans expel the Etruscan kings and begin the republic.

390 b.c. Celts attack and burn the city of Rome, then withdraw.

300s b.c. All of China is united for the first time under the Qin dynasty, which is followed by the Han dynasty. The Chinese finish constructing the Great Wall, built to protect their empire against warring tribes from the north. Buddhism spreads.

50s b.c. Caesar invades Britain.

The Parthians defeat the Romans at Carrhae, beginning a centuries-long series of conflicts between the Persian and Roman empires.

Julius Caesar conquers Gaul.

44 b.c. Caesar rules Rome's republic as dictator until his assassination on March 15.

Early Empire

27 b.c. The Senate transfers power to Octavian (also known as Augustus). This ends the republic and begins the period of the empire.

A.D. 98   Trajan takes power. Under his rule, the empire reaches its farthest borders.

105   In China, Tsai Lun invents paper.

117–138   During his reign, Hadrian changes the Roman army's purpose from offensive to defensive. He pulls back the empire's borders and reinforces them.

180   Marcus Aurelius, the last of the Five Good Emperors, dies, ending the period of prosperity known as the Pax Romana. The Antonine Plague ravages the empire. Aurelius's son, Commodus, becomes emperor.

LATE EMPIRE

193   The Severan Dynasty, a series of military emperors, starts with Septimius Severus and ends with the death of Alexander Severus.

220   China's Han dynasty ends.

224   The Sassanids defeat the Parthians and become rulers of the Persian Empire. They are a serious military threat to the Roman Empire.

235–284   The Roman Empire experiences fifty years of civil conflict. Many emperors during this period are killed by military factions.

284   Diocletian takes power and temporarily saves the Roman Empire. But his efforts to enrich the army place a heavy tax burden on the citizens.

286	Diocletian divides the empire into eastern and western halves.
305	Diocletian retires.
324	Constantine becomes ruler of the entire Roman Empire.
330	Constantine moves the empire's base from Rome to Constantinople, which he makes a Christian city.
337	Constantine dies after being baptized in the Christian church.
MID-300s	Huns invade Europe from the east, spreading terror and pushing other tribes toward the Roman Empire.
375–395	Reign of Theodosius I, the last effective leader of both halves of the Roman Empire.
376	Emperor Valens allows Goths to move into the Roman Empire and keep their own leaders.
378	Goths defeat the Romans at Adrianopolis, killing the Roman emperor Valens. The Goths' stunning victory demoralizes the Roman army, which never truly recovers from its losses.
402	Honorius, emperor of the western empire, moves its capital to Ravenna.
408	Honorius orders the execution of his barbarian

guardian, Stilicho, increasing hostilities between barbarians and Romans.

410–453 Under Alaric, the Goths sack the city of Rome. In 442 the empire gives up the province of Britain to a new barbarian group, the Saxons.

The Vandals take Carthage.

Attila rages through the empire but is stopped in Gaul by a Roman-Gothic army. In 453, Attila dies and the Huns scatter.

455 The Vandals, led by Gaiseric, attack Rome and destroy it again.

476 The last Roman emperor, Romulus Augustulus, is deposed by Odoacer, and the Western Roman Empire falls. Odoacer now rules Rome.

527 Justinian becomes emperor of the eastern empire and tries to restore the Roman Empire's lands and religion.

565 Justinian dies of natural causes.

1453 The Eastern Roman Empire is conquered by the Ottoman Turks.

GLOSSARY

ANCIENT CIVILIZATION: refers to known civilizations that flourished anytime between about 3,000 B.C. and A.D. 476. These civilizations include ancient Greece and Rome, as well as other societies that prospered around or near the Mediterranean Sea, such as the Assyrians, Egyptians, Israelites, and Persians. Other great civilizations developed in India, North and South America, and China.

ANCIENT WORLD: generally refers to the known world anytime between 3,000 B.C. to A.D. 476

ANTONINE PLAGUE: a deadly plague that ravished the Roman Empire during the reign of Marcus Aurelius (A.D.161–180). It killed approximately one-third of the empire's population, among them many soldiers of the Roman army. These deaths greatly weakened the military resources of the empire. The plague may have been the cause of Marcus Aurelius's death in A.D. 180. The source of this plague is not known.

ARCHAEOLOGY: the scientific study of ancient ruins and remains and what they reveal about ancient civilizations

BARBARIAN: the name given by Greeks and Romans to virtually anyone who did not speak Greek or was not a Roman citizen. The Romans expanded the meaning of the term to those who wanted to destroy the societies of the Greeks and Romans.

BYZANTINE EMPIRE: the eastern segment of the Roman Empire after the fall of the Western Roman Empire in A.D. 476. The name *Byzantine* comes from the ancient Greek city of Byzantium. The Roman emperor, Constantine, renamed the city Constantinople in A.D. 330. The Byzantine Empire lasted until 1453, when the Ottoman Turks took over Constantinople.

CHRISTIAN CHURCH: the early or ancient Christian church before Christianity became the official religion of the Roman Empire during the reigns of Constantine (A.D. 307–337) and Theodosius (A.D. 379–395). The earliest Christian church was conceived by the Jewish followers of Jesus of Nazareth.

CITY-STATE: a self-governing state consisting of a city and its surrounding territory

CLASSICAL WORLD: the world during the dominance of the Greek and Roman civilizations in the Mediterranean area (around 500 B.C. to A.D. 476). These two societies emphasized order, balance, and simplicity as characteristics of an ideal life.

ETRUSCANS: people living along the eastern coast of the Italian peninsula. Their monarchy dominated the Romans until around 500 B.C.

GERMANIC LANGUAGES: a group of related languages spoken by the barbarian tribes that migrated into present-day Europe. Most came from areas that are now

Scandinavia, Denmark, Germany, and Austria. The Celts (or Gauls) were the first to attack the Romans in 384 B.C.

INDO-EUROPEAN LANGUAGES: a family of related languages, including most European languages, in addition to languages of Iran, the Indian subcontinent, and parts of Asia

LATIN: the language spoken throughout the Roman Empire. Many modern languages, such as English, French, Spanish, and Portuguese, developed from Latin.

PAGAN: in modern times, this term is sometimes given to someone who is not a follower of the one God of Judaism, Christianity, or Islam. It also can refer to anyone who is nonreligious. In ancient Rome, "pagan" referred to followers of any of the many gods that were popular in the ancient world.

PAX ROMANA: "Roman Peace" (27 B.C.–A.D. 180); refers to the period of relative peace and prosperity enjoyed by Romans beginning with the reign of Octavian and ending with the death of Marcus Aurelius.

TETRARCHY: a country divided into four geographical or administrative parts

WESTERN CIVILIZATION: This is more of a philosophical than geographical term. Generally speaking, it defines those cultures that developed from the ancient cultures of Greece and Rome, including European and American cultures.

WHO'S WHO?

AUGUSTINE (A.D. 354–430) Aurelius Augustinus, from

Carthage in North Africa, was known as Augustine, or Saint Augustine of Hippo. He is famous for his role in the early Christian church and his religious writings, such as *The City of God* and *On Christian Learning*. He also wrote about the fall of Rome to the Goths in 410. Augustine died during the Vandal siege of Hippo Regius (Royal Horse), the North African city where he was bishop.

EUSEBIUS OF CAESAREA (A.D. 260–340) Eusebius, a Christian writer of many books, was appointed bishop of Caesarea in 314. In addition to his account of Diocletian's persecution of the Christians, he wrote an important history of the ancient world. He was also Constantine's biographer. Some scholars think Eusebius may have presented the emperor as more of a Christian than he really was. Eusebius wrote in Greek, not Latin.

FLAVIA MAXIMA FAUSTA (D. A.D. 326) Fausta was the wife of Emperor Constantine. She was also the daughter of Emperor Maximian, who plotted to overthrow Constantine. Constantine ordered Maximian's execution after Fausta revealed that her father was involved in a plot to overthrow the government. Fausta was also the sister of Maxentius, defeated by Constantine at the Milvian Bridge in A.D. 312.

GAISERIC (c. A.D. 399–c. 477) Gaiseric, also known as Genseric the Lame because he had difficulty walking, was king of the Vandals and Alans from 428 until 477. He was a continual threat to the Roman Empire in the fifth century. Known for his fondness for battle and aggression, he began conquering Roman North Africa in 429. He signed a treaty with Valentinian III in 435. In exchange for peace, the emperor freely gave Gaiseric the lands he had already taken by force. But when Valentinian died, Gaiseric invaded Carthage and took that too.

HELENA OF ILLYRICUM (D. A.D. 3) Helena was the

mother of Constantine. She and her son were abandoned by Constantine's father, Constantius Chlorus, for political reasons. Constantius was appointed caesar (assistant to the emperor) by Maximianus during Diocletian's tetrarchy. When Constantine grew up, he was reunited with his father and became emperor. As emperor, Constantine honored his mother by giving her the title of Augusta. As Augusta, Helena was able to give her son wise advice, becoming very influential in the governing of the empire. Known for her goodness and charity, she was made a saint by the Eastern Orthodox Church after her death.

JORDANES (A.D. 500s) Jordanes was the earliest known barbarian who wrote about the Goths. Little is known about Jordanes, but he was probably descended from an Alan family from the Roman province of Moesia in eastern Europe. He is also believed to have been a Christian convert. His book *The History and Origin of the Goths* is a summary of an earlier book written by a non-barbarian.

JOSEPHUS (C. A.D. 38–C. 95) Flavius Josephus, known as Josephus, was a Jewish writer and historian. He wrote many historical works, including a Jewish history in twenty volumes. He was decidedly favorable to the Romans, but he did write a strong argument against anti-Jewish attitudes. His last work was translated from Greek to Latin and is generally known as *Contra*. Josephus also wrote in Aramaic, an ancient language closely related to Hebrew and spoken by Jesus. Aramaic is still spoken in small communities in Syria, Iraq, Turkey, and Iran.

JULIA DOMNA (A.D. 170–217) Julia Domna was married to

the emperor Septimius Severus and accompanied him on all his military campaigns. She is thought to have been the most powerful woman in Roman history because of her influence over her husband. After Septimius died in 211, Julia tried to keep the peace between her sons, Caraculla and Geta, who both wanted sole power over the empire. Caraculla got it—by murdering his brother. Julia never forgave him, yet, during his frequent absences, she ran the government. Some historians believe that when Caraculla was killed by his own guards in 217, Julia planned to take over the throne herself and rule the empire. But she was already quite ill, possibly from breast cancer. Grieving for both her lost sons, she committed suicide in 217.

LEO I (c. A.D. 400–461) Leo I became the bishop of Rome (also known as the pope) in 440. He was an extremely important figure in the early Christian church and helped define its beliefs and government. His diplomatic skills also made him important to the Romans. In 452, he persuaded Attila the Hun not to destroy the city of Rome. Attila withdrew peacefully and went home. Leo also tried to stop Gaiseric (Genseric) and his Vandals from attacking Rome. He failed, but scholars think the damage the Vandals inflicted might have been worse if Leo I had not been involved.

PRISCUS (c. A.D. 400S) Priscus was considered an unusually objective eyewitness to fifth-century events during the reign of Theodosius II. Sent as a Roman official to meet with Attila the Hun, he attended a banquet hosted by the king of the Huns. In his rare personal account of Attila, Priscus described him as a man of cleanliness and humility, rather than of vicious and murderous intent.

PROCOPIUS (c. A.D. 500 TO AFTER 562) Born in Palestine, Procopius was a Greek historian and high official in Constantinople under the rule of Justinian I. Three of his books have survived. One is a study of buildings and art in

Constantinople. The other two are part of an eight-volume record of Justinian's reign, and a secret volume that could not have been made public during Procopius's life. This work, *Secret History*, tells what Procopius really thought of the emperor.

THEODORA OF CONSTANTINOPLE (A.D. 502–548)

Theodora was the beautiful and intelligent wife of the Byzantine Empire's ruler, Justinian I. She reigned together with her husband from 527 until she died in 548. She did much to improve the empire by helping Justinian manage many important building projects, including churches and public facilities. She gave shelter to women in need and encouraged her husband to pass laws that gave women more rights. Before she became empress, she was an actress who was famous for performing nude.

SOURCE NOTES

4 Cicero, Marcus Tullius, *Against Verres, The Verrine Orations*, trans. L. H. G. Greenwood, Loeb Classic Library (Cambridge, MA: Harvard University Press, 1935), p. 629.

5 Suetonius, *Life of Augustus xxi, xxii*, in Napthali Lewis and Meyer Reinhold, eds., *Roman Civilization Selected Readings, Volume II*, New York: Columbia University Press, 1955, 43–44.

15 Josephus, Time-Life. *What Was Life Like When Rome Ruled the World?* Alexandria, VA: Time-Life, Inc., 1997, 116.

15 Ibid.

19 Marcus Fabius Quintilian, *Orator's Education (Instutio Oratoria)* 12, in Greg Woolf, ed., *Cambridge Illustrated History of the Roman World*, Cambridge, UK: Cambridge University Press, 2003, 179.

19 Time-Life, 258.

22 Juvenal, *Satires*, in Lewis, 229.

24 *We Who are About to Die*, Chapter III, 2007, http://www .kurtsaxon.com/those_a_t _d/chapter03.htm (March 13, 2007).

25 Time-Life, 42.

27 Time-Life, 14111.

28 Ovid, *Metamorphosis Tales, Book III*, 2004, http://oaks .nvg.org/omb.html (March 23, 2007).

31 Dio Cassius, *Roman History, LXXI, xxvi 4*, in Lewis, 419.

33 Ibid., 419–20.

34–35 Ibid, 429.

36 Ibid, 423.

37 Ibid, 439.

40 Lewis, 439.

44 E. A. Thompson, *Romans and Barbarians: The Decline of Western Europe*. Madison, WI: University of Wisconsin Press, Ltd., 1982, 3–5.

47 Strabo McCullough, *Geographica*, translated by H. C. Hamilton and W. Falconer, London: George Bell & Sons, 1892, 8.

47 Ibid., 3.

55 Thompson, 5.

56 Dero A. Saunders, ed., *The Rise and Fall of the Roman Empire: The Portable Gibbon*, Edward Gibbon, New York: Viking Press, 206.

60 Aurelius Victor, *Lives of the Emperors, xxxix*, 17–48, abridged, in Lewis, 457.

61 Lacantius, *The Deaths of the Persecutors, vii,* in Lewis, 45.

67 Aurelius Victor, in Lewis, 456.

68–69 Eusebius, *Ecclesiastical Histories Translations and Reprints from the Original Sources of European History,* (Internet Medieval Source Book, *Diocletian: Edicts Against the Christians,* 1996) vol. 4, chap 1. 26–28 http://www.fordham.edu/halsall/source/persec1.html (March 21, 2007).

73 Ibid.

74 From the inscription on the Arch of Constantine, December 1999, http://penelope.uchicago.edu/Thayer/E/Gazetteer/Places/Europe/Italy/Lazio/Roma/Rome/Arch_of_Constantine/inscriptions.html (March 28, 2007).

76 D.G. Kousoulas, *The Life and Times of Constantine the Great,* Danbury, CT: Rutledge Books, Inc., 1997, 241.

85 Lewis, 456.

88 McCullough, 83.

92 Ibid., 121.

92–93 Ibid., 119.

95 Ibid., 127.

95 Ibid., 128.

96 Ibid., 134.

96 Ibid., 135.

98 Ibid., 138.

98–99 Ibid., 139.

99 Ibid.

99 Ibid., 141.

100 Ibid., 127.

101 Eunapius quoted in Thompson, 40.

109–110 Saunders, 607.

110 Ibid., 507–608.

110–111 Augustine, *The City of God,* in Chris Scarre, *The Penguin Historical Atlas of Ancient Rome.* (New York: Penguin Books, 1995), 132.

114 McCullough, "Negotiating and Dining with Attila," *Chronicles of the Barbarians: Firsthand Accounts of Pillage and Conquest, from the Ancient World to the Fall of Constantinople,* New York: Random House, 163.

118 William Yeats, First stanza from "The Second Coming," http://www.stfrancis.edu/en/yeats!.htm (March 28, 2007).

SELECTED BIBLIOGRAPHY

PRIMARY SOURCES

Cicero, Marcus Tullius. *Against Verres*, part 2, book 5, section 57. *The Verrine Orations*. Trans. by L. H. G. Greenwood. Loeb Classical Library. Cambridge, MA: Harvard University Press, 1935. These works include Cicero's famous use of the Roman proud statement, "I am a Roman citizen!"

Eusebius. *Ecclesiastical History*. Eusebius of Caesarea Project, 1998. http://www.ucalgary.ca/~vandersp/Courses/texts/eusebius/eusehe.html. Significant portions of this ancient historical account are available at the website of the University of Calgary.

Grant, Michael. *The Ancient Historians*. New York: Scribner's, 1970. This is a study, complete with portions of original writings, of the classical historians who wrote from 500 B.C. to A.D. 500, including Josephus, Caesar, and Suetonius.

Halsall, Paul. *Ancient History Sourcebook*. Internet History Sourcebook Project, 1999. http://www.fordham.edu/HALSALL/ancient/asbook.html. This website provides sourcebooks for the ancient, medieval, and modern periods and gives quick access to primary information. These sourcebooks also provide links to advanced research sites and to visual and aural resources.

Josephus, Flavius. *Jewish Antiquities*. Early Jewish Writings. Ed. Peter Kirby, 2006. http://www.earlyjewishwritings.com/. This is the most comprehensive collection of ancient Jewish documents available. Among other important documents, this site gives the full text of the Talmud and the Dead Sea Scrolls.

Lewis, Napthali, and Meyer Reinhold, editors. *Roman Civilization Selected Readings Volume II*. New York: Columbia University Press, 1955. Lewis and Reinhold tell the history of the Roman Empire by using ancient documents, writings, and orations from the Romans and other classical authors and historians. These primary sources include such famous works as Julius Caesar's *Gallic Wars* and Aurelius Victor's *Lives of the Romans.*

McCullough, David Willis. *Chronicles of the Barbarians: Firsthand Accounts of Pillage and Conquest, from the Ancient World to the Fall of Constantinople.* New York: Random House, 1998. This is a collection of primary sources relating the complex relationship between the Romans and the barbarians. It includes writings of classical Roman and Greek historians, such as Tacitus and Ammianus Marcellinus, as well as the Goth historian, Jordanes. In addition, it gives eyewitness accounts of such events as a banquet with Attila the Hun and the bloody battle of Adrianopolis.

Ovid. *Famous Quotes Throughout World History: Quotes from the Roman Empire.* Ed. David Sedivy. June 1, 2007. Highlands Ranch High School. June 11, 2007
http://mr_sedivy.tripod.com/quotes3.html.
Ovid was a great Roman poet and writer. He is most famous for his epic work, *Metamorphoses*, written in the early first century, which retells the history and traditional stories of classical Greece and Rome. He was also known for his clever remarks and love poems.

Pliny the Elder. *Natural History.* The Perseus Digital Library Project. Ed. Gregory R. Crane. June 12, 2007. Tufts University. June 11, 2007
http://www.perseus.tufts.edu/cgi-bin/ptext?lookup=Plin.+Nat.+toc.
This 37-volume encyclopedia of classical knowledge covers topics ranging from astronomy to the fine arts. Pliny died, of undetermined cause, while trying to rescue victims of the eruption of Mount Vesuvius in A.D. 79. His interest in the natural world was so intense that as he was dying, he dictated his observations on the scientific aspects of the eruption.

SECONDARY SOURCES

Adkins, Lesley, and Roy A. Adkins. *Handbook to Life in Ancient Rome.* New York: Oxford University Press, 1998.

Bowersock, G. W. ed., et al. *Late Antiquity: A Guide to the Postclassical World.* Cambridge, MA: Harvard University Press, 1999.

Browning, Robert. *Justinian and Theodora.* Piscataway, NJ: Gorgias Press, 2003.

Burns, Thomas S. *Barbarians within the Gates of Rome: A Study of Roman Military Policy and the Barbarians, ca. 375–425* A.D. Bloomington, IN: Indiana University Press, 1994.

Bury, B. *History of the Later Roman Empire.* New York: Dover, 1957.

Dorey, T. A., ed. *Latin Historians.* London: Routledge & Kegan Paul, Ltd., 1968.

Gibbon, Edward. *The Decline and Fall of the Roman Empire.* David Wormsley, ed. New York: Penguin, 2001.

Gies, Frances, and Joseph Gies. *Women in the Middle Ages.* New York: Thomas Y. Crowell Company, 1978.

Grant, Michael. *Constantine The Great: The Man and His Times.* New York: Charles Scribner's Sons, 1993.

———. *The World of Rome:* Cleveland, OH: World Publishing Company, 1960.

Heather, Peter. *The Fall of Rome: A New History of Rome.* New York: Oxford University Press, 2006.

Kousoulas, D. G. *The Life and Times of Constantine the Great.* Danbury, CT: Rutledge Books, Inc., 1997.

Lewis, Jone Johnson. "Theodora: Byzantine Empress," *Women in History.* 2006. http://womenshistory.about.com/library/bio/blbio_theodora.htm (Feb. 24, 2007).

Malcolm, Todd. *Everyday Life of the Barbarians: Goths, Franks and Vandals.* New York: G.P. Putnam's Sons, 1972.

Matz, David. *Daily Life of the Ancient Romans.* Westport, CT: Greenwood Press, 2002.

Newark, Tim. *The Barbarians, Warriors & Wars of the Dark Ages*. Dorset, UK: Blandford Press, 1985.

Randers-Pehrsen, Justine Davis. *Barbarians and Romans: The Birth Struggle of Europe*, A.D. *400–700*. Norman, OK: University of Oklahoma Press, 1983.

Saunders, Dero A. *The Portable Gibbon: The Decline and Fall of the Roman Empire* by Edward Gibbon. New York: Penguin Books, 1977.

Scarre, Chris. *The Penguin Historical Atlas of Ancient Rome*. New York: Penguin Books, 1995.

Starr, Chester G. *A History of the Ancient World*. New York: Oxford University Press, 1983.

Thompson, E. A. *Romans and Barbarians: The Decline of Western Europe*. Madison, WI: University of Wisconsin Press, Ltd., 1982.

Time-Life. *What Was Life Like When Rome Ruled the World?* Alexandria, VA: Time-Life, 1997.

Todd, Malcolm. *Everyday Life of the Barbarians: Goths, Franks and Vandals*. New York: G.P. Putnam's Sons, 1972.

Usher, Stephen. *The Historians of Greece and Rome*. New York: Tarplinger Publishing, 1969.

Wells, Peter S. *The Barbarians Speak: How the Conquered Peoples Shaped Roman Europe*. Princeton, NJ: Princeton University Press, 1999.

Woolf, Greg, ed. *Cambridge Illustrated History of the Roman World*. Cambridge, UK: Cambridge University Press, 2003.

FURTHER READING

Behnke, Alison. *Italy in Pictures*. Minneapolis: Twenty-First Century Books, 2003.

Burghusen, Joan. *Daily Life in Ancient and Modern Rome*. Minneapolis: Lerner Publications, 1999.

DuTemple, Lesley A. *The Colosseum*. Minneapolis: Twenty-First Century Books, 2003.

Kleeman, Terry, and Tracy Barrett. *The Ancient Chinese World*. New York: Oxford University Press, 2005.

Markel, Rita J. *Your Travel Guide to Ancient Rome*. Minneapolis: Twenty-First Century Books, 2004.

Mathews-Green, Frederica. *At the Corner of East and Now: A Modern Life in Ancient Christian Orthodoxy*. New York: Penguin Books, 2000.

Nardo, Don. *The Decline and Fall of the Roman Empire*. San Diego: Lucent Books, 1998.

Petras, Kathryn, and Ross Petras. *Mythology: Tales & Legends of the Gods*. New York: Workman Press, 1998.

Trustees of the British Museum. *Ancient Roman Knowledge Cards*. Rohnert Park, CA: Pomegranate Publications, 2003.

WEBSITES

Empire: An Overview of the Ancient World Empires
http://regentsprep.org/Regents/global/themes/diversity/empires.cfm
This website provides a helpful chart on ancient empires that developed around the Mediterranean and along the Silk Road.

"Finding a Lost Emperor in a Clay Pot," at *Doug Smith's Ancients*
http://dougsmith.ancients.info/aurelian.html
This website shows the coins issued during the late Roman Empire. It also makes visitors aware of how valuable ancient Rome's coins are as primary sources to historians.

Illustrated History of the Roman Empire
http://www.roman-empire.net/maps/map-empire.html
This website has good topographical maps that show Rome compared to other empires, the ancient city of Rome, and the modern-day countries now occupying territory that was once part of the Roman Empire.

"The Invasion of Britain" *UNRV History*
http://www.unrv.com/fall-republic/britain-invasion.php
This site describes Caesar's invasions of the British Isles and the barbarians he met there.

"Italy and Rome Picture Gallery" at *Historylink101.com*
http://historylink102.com/italy/roman-forum-2.htm
This is a photo gallery of Roman architecture, including the Colosseum, Palatine Hill, and the Roman forum.

Lo, Larry. *Ancient Scripts.com*.
http://www.ancientscripts.com/alphabet.html.

Pictures of Rome
http://www.abcroma.com/Monumenti/MonumentiFoto_i.asp?N=2
This site gives good views of Rome's Arch of Constantine with the Colosseum in the background.

"Rome: Engineering an Empire" at *History.Com video gallery*.
http://www.history.com/media.do?action=clip&id=rome_colosseum
This website has a great video tour of Rome's Colosseum.

Trade Between the Empires of Asia and Rome
http://www.metmuseum.org/toah/hd/silk/hd_silk.htm
This Metropolitan Museum of Art site gives an overview of the empires of Rome's ancient world and the Silk Road, including the Han dynasty of China, the Persian Empire (both Parthian and Sassanid eras), and the Kushan Empire of India.

INDEX

ABOUT THE AUTHOR

Rita J. Markel's stories and historical articles for children and teens have appeared in magazines and books. She has written on topics such as rock legend Jimi Hendrix, President Grover Cleveland, America's Old West, ancient Rome, the Gee-Bee racing planes, and the U.S. Army Camel Corps. She lives in Boise, Idaho.

PHOTO ACKNOWLEDGMENTS

The images in this book are used with the permission of: © Bettmann/CORBIS, pp. 5, 7, 109; The Art Archive/Museo Prenestino Palestrina/Dagli Orti (A), p. 8; © Laura Westlund/Independent Picture Service, pp. 12, 42, 58, 107; The Art Archive/National Museum Bucharest/Dagli Orti (A), p. 13; © Oxford Events Photography/Alamy, p. 14; © British Museum/Art Resource, NY, p. 16; © British Museum/HIP/Art Resource, NY, p. 20; © Robert Campbell/SuperStock, p. 23; The Art Archive/Museo Capitolino Rome/Dagli Orti, pp. 30, 144; © Bildarchiv Preussischer Kulturbesitz/Art Resource, NY, p. 34; The Art Archive/Museo Nazionale Palazzo Altemps Rome/Dagli Orti, pp. 41, 65; © Hulton Archive/Getty Images, p. 46; © Erich Lessing/Art Resource, NY, pp. 48, 50, 83, 103; The Art Archive/Historiska Muséet Stockholm/Dagli Orti (A), p. 53; © Alinari Archives/The Image Works, p. 57; The Art Archive/Museo di Capodimonte, Naples/Dagli Orti (A), p. 68; © Araldo de Luca/CORBIS, p. 69; © Giovanni Guarino/Alamy, p. 71; The Art Archive/Jan Vinchon Numismatist Paris/Dagli Orti, pp. 75, 93; © Gianni Giansanti/Sygma/CORBIS, p. 76; © Burstein Collection/CORBIS, p. 77; The Art Archive/Dagli Orti, pp. 79, 84, 120, 134; The Art Archive/Musée du Louvre Paris/Dagli Orti, p. 86; The Art Archive/Biblioteca Capitolare Vercelli/Dagli Orti, p. 101; The Art Archive/Tesoro del Duomo Aosta/Dagli Orti, p. 104; © Scala/Art Resource, NY, pp. 113, 145; © Kean Collection/Hulton Archive/Getty Images, p. 115; © Archivo Iconografico, S.A./CORBIS, pp. 122, 123; The Art Archive/Galleria degli Uffizi Florence/Dagli Orti, p. 143.

Front cover: © Alinari/Art Resource, NY.